RESOLVE

RESOLVE

A JOURNEY WEIGHTED BY GRIEF, DISRUPTED BY TRUTH, AND AWAKENED TO PURPOSE

MITCH BAKKER

credo
house publishers

ISBN (Hardcover): 978-1-62586-163-4
ISBN (Softcover): 978-1-62586-164-1
ISBN (Study Guide): 978-1-62586-165-8
ISBN (Ebook): 978-1-62586-166-5
ISBN (Audio): 978-1-62586-167-2

Cover design by Mitch Bakker and Justin Heap (justinpheap.co)
Interior design by Sharon VanLoozenoord
Editing by Rachel E. Newman

Printed in the United States of America

First Edition

mitchbakker.com

CONTENTS

INTRODUCTION

This book, *Resolve,* contains fifty-seven reflections written on or before I completed my fifty-seventh year of life—a pivotal year for me as it was the age my father, Karl, went home to be with the Lord, some twenty-five years ago now. Fifty-seven was a milestone I was not looking forward to, but it has caused me to turn my gaze upward to reflect on my faith journey. Dad's life and love has impacted me in so many ways, right up to this very day. He was a man who loved God and the Scriptures, so often quoting them aloud. One of his favorite verses of Scripture was, "A merry heart doeth good like a medicine: but a broken spirit drieth the bones" (Prov. 17:22 KJV). It has been enriching to reflect on Dad throughout this project.

The brevity of life crystalized before me as I began to turn the pages and chapters that my father never did. What I did not anticipate, however, was the sense of urgency that would come from being held in the middle space between the deaths of both my parents—urgency to uncover and share disruptive truth, urgency to make my life mean more, urgency to steward well the time that I have left on this earth. My fifty-seventh year became not only a memoriam to the days my father never had, but a year of pulling at the threads of my journey through grief, failures, tragedies, grace, and joy that have been woven through my life story. It became a year dedicated not just to understanding what death would mean for me, but what my life would mean for others.

The undeniable truths that emerged over that year have become this book—a collection of my own stories, scriptural reflections, and modern day parables. In unique ways, each reflection explores knowing Christ through my journey and recognizes his call to action, a call to love and serve the marginalized that requires a proper alignment of stewardship, values, and obedience. It is also an invitation to receive the grace, mercy, and love offered by Christ.

Resolve is about more than a certain year, a landmark birthdate, or a date range on a headstone, it's about being halted—suspended in time long enough to look backward over my journey, in order to look forward with intention toward eternity.

Now, each successive day is more precious to me, as it is one day closer to my last. With that in mind, I ask myself, "What is my legacy? What is my impact? How do I want to be remembered?" As I waded through a year heavy with grief, self-realization, and conviction, I was also overcome with a desire to bring others along with me into a life more fully devoted to God's truth, mission, and vision for this Earth. Resolve is about more than a certain year, a landmark birthdate, or a date range on a headstone, it's about being halted—suspended in time long enough to look backward over my journey, in order to look forward with intention toward eternity.

SUPERNATURAL
LIFE AND DEATH

1

In Between

As I sat in the room, time slowed. The woman who had brought me into the world was leaving it. Losing a loved one is hard, especially when it's a parent. Someone who has been with you from your very first day, from your very first breath. On this, her last day, she lay next to me, despondent and fighting for every breath.

In these moments, reflection is so natural. I reflected on my life and on the lives of my parents, Marie and Karl. It had been twenty-five years since Dad passed away, and in a few days, I was turning fifty-seven, the age he was when he died. Twenty-five years had come and gone so quickly. I looked at Mom and realized she was twenty-five years older than me. I was in this mysterious middle space, simultaneously looking backward and forward twenty-five years.

It's so easy to go through our days feeling like life will continue as it always has—until a moment like this, and suddenly you're jolted with the stark realization that life is ultimately brief, brief and winding down to your last breath. I was hit hard with the conviction that if I was granted twenty-five more years, they would not be the same as the last. They would include old age and a dwindling of my energy, my strength, and perhaps my faculties. I was experiencing a crisis of sorts, a life crisis, to be sure. My own fifty-seventh birthday falling within the week Mom died added to my sense of urgency.

It's so easy to go through our days feeling like life will continue as it always has—until a moment like this, and suddenly you're jolted with the stark realization that life is ultimately brief, brief and winding down to your last breath.

She took her last breath on a Sunday morning. My sisters, Karyl and Karyn, were with me, along with my nieces Shawna and Kat. This was the first time I had been physically present at a person's passing. It was surreal. What was it was like for her to be free from her body and to immediately have her mind restored as she was carried into the presence of her Lord? I walked outside and wept. She was my mother, and I was her son. I knew I could have been a better son, could have expressed my love for her more, called her more, visited more. So many things I could have done better, more, differently. But she knew I loved her, and I knew she loved me. That has to be enough now. Mom was very independent and was so content with her life. I loved and, in some ways, envied that about her. She rarely complained and never expressed disappointment in me but was always proud of me. She lived a beautiful, uncomplicated life filled with joy and love for the people in it.

We had a simple graveside service along the perimeter of the cemetery. After the service, I stayed and watched a yellow backhoe maneuver through the snow and lift the vault with her casket sealed inside. The still, frigid air was broken up by the soft purr of the motor and the crackling of the frozen ground beneath the tires as she was carried over and lowered into her final resting place beside Dad. I imagined the two of them, years earlier, dreaming about their lives and the promising road ahead: the family they would raise, the vacations, the accomplishments, the joy in seeing their children's achievements. And now it all had come to this, a cold winter day, their lifeless bodies together laid to rest. It was over. Time had run its course. They had succumbed to the same destiny all of us face. Laid to rest under a bare, snow-covered maple tree, now living only through their children and grandchildren. Would they be remembered properly on this side of the grave?

Twelve years earlier, I had taken my son David to see his grandpa Karl's grave. We were amazed when we approached it and saw the headstone. The cemetery was covered in a blanket of snow, yet his side of the headstone was completely dry. And there were no footprints in the snow indicating that someone had been there to clear it. Was this a sign? It was to us. A simple miracle and reminder that while life was moving along for the living, there was also a whole eternal realm that was anything but resting, a small signal that all was well on the other side of the grave. My father touched us that morning as we came to pay our respects and remember his life.

It was my mom's death on December 10, 2017, that awoke me anew to the brevity of life. I felt it deep in my core. Mom had passed, and I was running out of time. The race was on!

> Do you not know that in a race all the runners
> run, but only one gets the prize? Run in such a
> way as to get the prize. Everyone who competes
> in the games goes into strict training. They do it
> to get a crown that will not last, but we do it to
> get a crown that will last forever. Therefore I do
> not run like someone running aimlessly; I do
> not fight like a boxer beating the air. No, I strike
> a blow to my body and make it my slave so that
> after I have preached to others, I myself will not
> be disqualified for the prize. (1 Cor. 9:24–27)

2

What Now?

They gathered around Jesus as he spoke, not realizing these would be his final words. The worst was over, and they took comfort in what he said, especially now, now that he had risen from the grave. Now he would establish his kingdom on earth—or so they thought. He spoke of a Spirit baptism and the timing of the future kingdom, which was known and set by his Father. After his clarification and instructions, he paused, looked up, stretched out his arms, and slowly ascended upward into the sky (Acts 1:9). They never saw him again. He left them with his words and, later, his Spirit: the Holy Spirit that would take up residence within them.

Jesus's last miracle, his ascension, left a lasting impression on them all. They stood speechless, each of them gazing into the sky, hoping for one last glimpse, when they were startled by an unfamiliar voice: "Men of Galilee, why do you stand here looking into the sky? This same Jesus, who has been taken from you into heaven, will come back in the same way you have seen him go into heaven" (Acts 1:11).

This was the beginning of the new age of the New Testament church. The two men dressed in white who suddenly appeared to the apostles were sent by God to encourage them with a clear message: Jesus will return in the same way. Their last question to Jesus, "Lord, are you at this time going to restore the kingdom to Israel?" was answered by the angels in their midst as both a no (not now) and a yes (at a future time). "In the same way, he will return to establish and restore his kingdom." Meanwhile, they were to get to work. To this day, that work continues—the work of proclamation through words and through acts of service, caring for those in need, the application of his words.

These acts of service were so important that when it was learned that certain widows were being overlooked in the daily distribution of food, the Twelve gathered all the disciples together and said, "It would not be right for us to neglect the ministry of the word of God in order to wait on tables. Brothers and sisters, choose seven men from among you who are known to be full of the Spirit and wisdom" (Acts 6:2–3). Acts of service, in this case the distribution of food, were so important that only those known to be full of the Spirit and wisdom would be chosen to carry out this ministry.

Additionally, an unspeakable generosity was evident among them. Selling and sharing what was theirs was second nature to these new Spirit-filled believers (Acts 2:45). Not just second nature, but literally a *new* nature, born from above and now resident within. It was none other than Jesus's nature, his Spirit, the same Spirit that empowered Jesus as he fed, healed, and cared for those in his midst. He was now at work within his disciples and all new converts, carrying out his work through them, and today through us.

Jesus now lives in the supernatural, in us and through us. He is supernatural and yet was born a natural man, lived a natural life, and experienced a natural death. His death was grueling, yet he never called on his Father or the angels to intervene, even when the pain increased. Jesus came to offer himself up for us and to take a punishment he did not deserve; he took it for us in bodily form. All of that changed after his resurrection! His resurrection was supernatural, as he was released from the natural world that he had subjected himself to for thirty-three years.

Jesus left the earth and will return in the same way he left, descending from above to establish his kingdom. Through his Spirit, he descended at Pentecost and is very much alive among us, through all who believe his message. His Spirit will be received throughout the ages and evidenced by unity, love, and generosity expressed by believers. Until he returns, we are called to walk like he walked because we have the same power through the same Spirit. A power that can only be experienced through his love.

Until he returns, we are called to walk like he walked because we have the same power through the same Spirit.

> Therefore he is able to save completely those
> who come to God through him, because he
> always lives to intercede for them. (Heb. 7:25)

3

Those Clouds!

It was pleasant and partly sunny on Friday, March 27, 1992, when my dad went home to be with Jesus. Dad was hospitalized and recovering from a pulmonary embolism, but his prognosis was good. Earlier that day, his doctor had informed him he would be releasing him on Sunday. Wonderful news for a young fifty-seven-year-old who was relatively healthy. My sister Karyn was with him to celebrate the news of his discharge. Dad had spent more than his share of time lying in bed and was practically crawling the walls of hospital rooms with an eagerness to get out. He was looking forward to returning to normalcy.

From his bed, Dad gazed out the window and took note of the clouds in the sky. These weren't just any old clouds, though. There was something special about them. He called out to Karyn to come and look with him. "Karyn, do you see those clouds?"

She obliged and stared out the window, seeing nothing but very normal clouds in the sky.

With assurance in his voice, Dad proclaimed, "Why, those are the exact same clouds that Jesus came on to get Marvin! The exact same ones!"

Karyn looked at him, trying not to ruin the moment yet having to admit she didn't see what he saw or what it had to do with Uncle Marvin, our father's older brother.

Surprised she had never heard the story, Dad went on to tell Karyn how his parents (my grandparents) had snuck him into the hospital to visit his very ill brother who was battling leukemia. Marvin was seven and Dad was five. While Dad was next to the bed, Marvin told him to look out the window as he exclaimed, "Jesus is coming on those clouds!" Marvin died shortly thereafter.

Karyn was touched by Dad's recollection. Little did she (or he) know this was foreshadowing, for just a few hours later, Dad suffered another clot and went home to be with the Lord.

Had Dad seen Jesus in the clouds as he was sitting next to Marvin so many years ago?

I assume he hadn't, just as Karyn didn't. It was only when his own time drew near that the curtains were pulled back to reveal the hidden reality of the afterlife, the eternal. In that moment, Dad recognized the clouds that Marvin had experienced, as he was now the one peering into the supernatural, a view that bridges past, present, and future.

> All believers alive today have become children in waiting for that glorious day when we too will be carried by the same Jesus, in the same power, to be in the same place.

All believers alive today have become children in waiting for that glorious day when we too will be carried by the same Jesus, in the same power, to be in the same place. All who know Christ look forward to his return. I know he is returning for me, to carry me home on those same celestial clouds.

"This same Jesus, who has been taken
from you into heaven [wrapped in clouds],
will come back in the same way you have
seen him go into heaven." (Acts 1:11)

4

A Letter to Julie

In February of 1999, our friend Julie lost her father. She was devastated; her father's death was so sudden, so unexpected. It was a number of years removed from Dad's passing, but I could still relate. His passing felt like yesterday. In many ways it still does. I wrote this letter to comfort her during that time.

Julie,

This letter is my perspective on my journey since my father's death and in some ways the journey that lies before you. A view to aid, comfort, and perhaps help you mark the path that lies ahead.

I remember how strong I was at my father's funeral and how special God's grace and presence were to me during that time.

Immediately after his death, I was so shaken in my faith but was comforted within twenty-four hours. I recall thinking, where is he? I mean, really, where is he right now? All my life I had believed in Christ, but could what I had believed hold up now? I wasn't so sure. This was my dad, not some distant acquaintance down the street. This was a man who's not supposed to check out at fifty-seven. This was the grandfather who was supposed to watch my kids grow up and be there for them, help guide them, encourage them, love them, and influence them along the way. How could Christ have allowed his sudden departure?

I received James Dobson's monthly letter in the mail from Focus on the Family the day after my father's death. That month he chose to share about the death of his own father and grandfather. In it he shared a poem that hit the mark of my dad's life. A poem that was recited at my father's funeral. The storm of my emotions, questions, and doubts was met with a supernatural response from a heavenly Father who was gracious enough to let me know it was okay and that in all things he was in control. He confirmed in my soul, without a shadow of doubt, that Dad was in his arms and that one day Dad would hold me and embrace me again. I needed desperately to know this, and God delivered through the James Dobson letter. In the letter, Dr. Dobson wrote about the passage of his father and the certainty he had of seeing our loved ones on the other side, recognizing them and embracing them. Those words were the answers to the specific issues weighing heavy on my heart. God also gave me so many special promises in his Word as confirmation of his sovereign and loving control of his child's future and hope.

It wasn't long after my father's death that the feelings of God's grace, presence, and warmth started to dim. God's grace is like that. It's the strongest when we need it the most, but our sense of his presence often fades like an anesthetic wearing off and exposing the pain. Our sense of his presence isn't always there, even though we know he is.

First I was hit with the sense of permanence. In the beginning it's easier to take the death of a loved one because your subconscious mind believes they are coming back. It's like saying goodbye to someone very close who is going away on a long trip. Just as you start to really miss them, they return. We were not wired to handle death, and this will become abundantly clear to you as more time passes. My subconscious was expecting him back, yet he never came back. I hit a wall at that point. I remember feeling as lonely as I have ever felt, with no one to comfort me. No one could. I resented the world for going on when I was in such deep sorrow. I resented the fact I had to go on when I felt like dying. I would jog to my father's grave (which was three to four miles from our home at the time) after work and lie on it weeping for extended periods of time. I didn't want to accept he was gone. I wanted my best friend back. The grieving and weeping were a healthy cleansing. Allow yourself this expression of grief. Let it move through you so you can move beyond it.

I would call his home number during the day, like I used to. He never answered. I knew he wouldn't. I would call anyway and let it ring and ring, holding out hope he would pick up the phone and life would resume as it had before. I couldn't accept the permanence. That's the hardest part. I wanted one more talk, one more hug, one more anything.

A few things did happen along the way, things I share with only a select few. One such event happened when I brought my mom to Calvary's Easter service. Not long after we sat down in the pew, I felt the strong sense of my father next to me. It wasn't just a faint feeling. It was real. I actually felt him next to me in the empty space to my right. I felt his arm around me, and I saw that familiar smile—an expression of his pride in me. I cannot explain how I saw it as I was looking ahead. I saw it in my mind's eye or in my soul. I felt his approval that I was caring for and looking after Mom. I could almost hear him say, "I'm proud of you, buddy." I never felt him again or sensed his presence in that way, but I will always treasure that one last time. Whether imagined or real makes no difference.

I have had many dreams with Dad in them. These, too, have been extremely comforting. Some of my dreams have come at difficult decision points, times I would have relied on my dad to help me through. I was able to ask key questions in those dreams and remember his answers in the morning. These are gifts that I have treasured in my heart. Not frequent, only a few, but rich nonetheless.

As time has passed, the pain and sting of his death has diminished and, thankfully, been replaced with a sweet remembrance of a wonderful man who, in a strange and marvelous way, lives within me. I now feel him living in me unlike anything I'd ever experienced when he was alive. I want to pass him on to my children, and I now realize that it is possible! I often say to my boys, "That's what Papa would say" or "You know where I learned that?" I find myself tickling them the way he tickled me or doing the silly little things that marked our time and intimacy together.

My love for my father in large part grew out of his caring enough to be there, to spend the time. I realize now what a special gift this time was. I took it for granted, this sacrifice of love. To him it was no sacrifice at all. I knew it wasn't out of obligation that he wanted to be with me; it was because he loved me more than the thousand other things he could be doing at the time. Somehow he was able to mark relationship building as his highest and most important calling. I don't feel I can measure up to that with my boys, but with God's grace I will attempt to.

My father passed away unexpectedly, as did yours. He was supposed to make a full recovery and had no life-threatening symptoms at the time. Then God took him. My sister Karyn was with him in the hospital at the time. My dad had gotten up to go to the bathroom, and as he was returning to his bed, he couldn't catch his breath. He tried to comfort Karyn by saying, "It's okay. I'll be alright." She knew better and called a nurse, who at the sight of my father immediately sounded the stat alarm. He had a severe blood clot that would take his life within minutes. As the staff ushered him into the bed and her out of the room, he was looking at Karyn out of the corner of his eye saying, "It's okay, honey. I'm going to be okay." Those were the last words he spoke to her. The intern at his side drawing his blood knew he was gone by its dark color. He later told us my father's last words as he looked upward were, "I'm going now."

I've often pondered the journey my father took in those last moments. My last time with him was a few days earlier when I'd eaten dinner at his bedside, he and I chatting as if we had all the time in the world. I still remember the topics: Billy Graham, Michigan basketball, and another very interesting topic—death. My good friend Dave Potter had told me about a near-death experience his father had. The timing of his telling it to me and my relaying it to my father in our last moments together was somewhat providential. I told my father about Mr. Potter feeling himself leaving his body and heading for a light with a wonderful sense of peace and the presence of God. Little did I know that within seventy-two hours my father would be taking that journey and God was even then preparing him for the trip.

God's hand is always present in the lives of his children.

When I got word my father had taken a turn for the worse, I ran to my car and headed to the hospital. I was thinking, *Is this the day God has chosen to take him?* I tried to dismiss the thought, but it kept flooding back. I remember stepping out of my car and looking up at the sky. Had Dad already taken that journey? When I got inside, I embraced my sisters and mother in the small cafeteria. Not long after that, two doctors with their heads hung low came down the hall to deliver the message I never wanted to hear. We cried and cried. I was numb, really not having a clue what this meant or what I was in for.

As terrible as this may sound, the only word that seemed to fit at the time was *shit.* I sat alone against the wall and said that word over and over and over again.

They allowed us to spend some time with him before taking him away. That was actually a very special time. One last time to feel his rough, calloused hands and touch him while he was still soft and warm and seemed very much alive, just asleep. What was minutes in that room now seems like hours as I reflect back.

I try to imagine his last journey. I've gotten to the place I can almost see it: his entering into the kingdom of heaven and being met with the loving and outstretched arms of his Savior. I can see the tears falling from his cheeks as he turns and sees those who have gone before him. He hugs and embraces his brother Marvin, who passed away at the age of seven, and his sister Sally. I can see him being shown around the splendor of heaven and beginning the time-less process of being reacquainted and reunited with those from so long ago. He is happy. That brings me joy.

I still miss him so. You see, my dad changed as I grew older. He went from being my dad to being a close friend. He became like a brother to me. He would often call me

Ken (his brother) by accident, followed by an apology and this statement: "I can't help it. You seem more like a brother to me than a son."

Dad's gone and life goes on. Life's not as it was, and it will never be the same. You can't replace those who are so dear. It makes heaven seem closer and earth less my home. My memories are mostly sweet now, and the bitter sting is gone. I loved him deeply and have paid a big price for the depth of my love. How much easier it would have been had we not been close. I would not trade the pain and the sting for a distant relationship. Love is that way; we are hurt the most when we love the deepest, but in the end, there is a priceless, eternal reward for our labors of love.

> *You can't replace those who are so dear. It makes heaven seem closer and earth less my home.*

There are so many emotions and events I would love to share, but there are too many to recount. The first year is the hardest. Feelings of regret and "if onlys" plague me at times. Not regrets over words or our relationship (thankfully). But I replay the illness, thinking if only I had done this or that or spoken to his doctors more. Anger at the hospital staff for allowing someone who was admitted with a blood clot to get up and walk around. Regret that I couldn't have helped my father more in his passage from this life to the next. You see, a week before he died, my father expressed his fear of dying and asked me to help him. I fear I didn't help him enough. The list goes on. I've had to let it all go and let God be sovereign. God wanted my father to go home and that's that. I'm certain our fathers have met by now. I imagine them comparing notes on their joyous relationships down here and anxiously awaiting our reunion.

5

Uncomplicated Faith

The sun beat down on my sister's long, blonde hair, pulled back in a ponytail to keep it out of her eyes—eyes that burned with sweat while she planted tree after tree, moving gracefully across the uneven terrain and rolling hills of Doyle Hall's farmland. One by one, she carefully pulled each tiny pine seedling—red, white, and spruce—out of the box and set it into the shallow groove cut through the rich soil. Over one million in all, planted over the five years she and Doyle toiled together.

Karyn Lee was a twenty-five-year-old city girl transplanted into the countryside of Kalkaska, Michigan, living in a light-blue farmhouse with her husband, Randy, finding work where she could. She was never one to shy away from hard labor, and, like the trees she planted, she would naturally sink deep into the lives and relationships of those whose paths she crossed. This happened with even the unlikeliest folks, like her neighbor, a crusty, old farmer named Doyle, who in time became her boss, her friend, and a father figure.

She had a strong, uncomplicated faith and was not shy or ashamed to discuss it. Her faith was not just an aspect of her life; it was her life, and it defined who she was. To know her was to know her faith. She lived an open-book life that was as refreshing as the cool country air on Doyle's farm.

> Her faith was not just an aspect of her life; it was her life, and it defined who she was.

Doyle would keep to himself as a quiet, nose-to-the-grindstone farmer. My sister, the young city girl looking for work, was quite the opposite. Karyn was willing to do anything, even if it meant fighting through the sweltering heat with burning muscles from planting trees for hours on end. The heat and the work required frequent breaks, and it was during these rest times that Karyn planted the seeds that mattered most to her: relational seeds for the soul.

These conversations were completely outside of Doyle's comfort zone, outside of even his past experience. To be talking on a break was new territory, but to go beyond the surface was an uncomfortable exposure he did not see coming and certainly did not welcome. To Doyle, faith was personal. How dare anyone discuss it in the open air? Even a harmless, blonde-haired, blue-eyed Dutch girl should keep these thoughts to herself. What Doyle did not know, though, was that he was the object of Karyn's work, not the silly little seedlings. Nor could Doyle know that with each little tree she was planting, she was also praying and claiming Acts 16:31 for him: "Believe in the Lord Jesus, and you will be saved—you and your household."

In time, little by little, Doyle opened up. Initially it was in a confrontational way.

"I'm an atheist," he said, proudly at first. But he quickly retreated to, "Do you hate me for that?" For as much as Doyle wanted to hold on to the ground of his belief, or lack thereof, he also did not want to offend or damage his relationship with

Karyn. She was special to him, and he didn't have much that was special in his simple, hardworking country life.

Karyn simply said, "I don't hate you. I'm praying for you."

Conversations ebbed and flowed. Most days Doyle was closed and guarded, but on occasion, he would open up and expose his thoughts.

Karyn was delighted one day when Doyle blurted out, "I'm no longer an atheist. I'm an agnostic."

He went on to explain he had given much thought to Karyn's objection to his atheistic belief: how could he, surrounded by the miracles of life, new growth, and the wonder of nature, deny the existence of God? Her simple yet profound objection to his lifelong belief churned repeatedly in his mind. No one had ever cared to challenge him, let alone to understand what he believed in the first place. To Karyn, this was progress, slow and steady; a seed had begun to grow.

Future conversations were more challenging.

"Christians are not good people!" Doyle was insistent.

Karyn would just smile. "Oh Doyle, you can always find reasons to not believe, but in the end, you are only responsible for you."

Doyle could not object to Karyn's wise and straightforward retort. Conversational seeds connected to the powerful prayers of this persistent young woman were finding their way into his soul. He would open up briefly and then retreat for days of quiet contemplation.

"I'm a good person. I've lived a good life. Why do I need Jesus?"

"Doyle, you can't earn your way to salvation. Salvation is only through faith in Jesus's perfect life and death on the cross for your sins and mine."

More conversations ensued, many seeming insignificant but each one having an effect, a cumulative effect.

It was in the fifth year of their working relationship that Doyle began to complain of headaches. This was unusual for a man who did not complain about anything, ever. Karyn was concerned and encouraged him to go to the doctor, knowing that would be a last resort for him.

It was in the early-morning hour when Karyn opened the door to his house. David, Doyle's son, stood stoically delivering the news that Karyn had secretly feared: "Dad has a cancerous brain tumor."

Unable to contain her emotions, she openly wept. Doyle's condition was so severe he would not be returning home until after surgery. After a number of days, Doyle did return home, but the prognosis was bleak. His new normal was frequent visits to clinics for chemotherapy. Karyn would take his wife, Beverly, to support groups, all part of the process no one desires.

It had been three weeks since the diagnosis and Doyle's deterioration was rapid. Karyn woke up sweating, panicked. Was this a dream, a nightmare, or a premonition? Her vision was of Doyle in a large field, all alone. She could see from his expression he was afraid, lonely, and lost. She attempted to go to him, to comfort him, but was unable to. He had made the choices that put him in this place.

The divine nature of this dream created a renewed sense of urgency within her. She dressed quickly and raced down to see Doyle, her heart beating rapidly. After some small talk with Beverly, she asked Doyle if he wanted to go out back and keep her company while she picked some rhubarb. Doyle obliged, holding on to Karyn while she walked with him to the back yard and positioned him in his worn-out lawn chair. Shoots of rhubarb sprung from the ground, ready to be harvested and made into pie—his favorite.

"So have you been giving more thought to our talks, Doyle?"

"Which ones?"

"Um, the ones about Jesus!"

Doyle just looked ahead with a blank stare as if nothing was registering. Karyn could no longer contain herself. She got down on one knee, tears streaming down her face, and looked straight into Doyle's eyes.

"I want to be with you in heaven," she said. "I cannot stand the thought of you not being there!"

Doyle, always the peacemaker, responded, "It's okay, yes, I thought about it. But please, Karyn, don't cry." His voice was weak, he was visibly shaken by her tears as he reached out to comfort her.

But Karyn knew it would not be okay until he had made peace with Christ and was found in him. Doyle was as stubborn as he was caring, which created a restlessness within him as he sought for normality within a body that was no longer obliging. Karyn looked at him, in his weak, weathered condition and wondered if her prayers would be answered in the short time he had left.

A few days passed and Karyn left for a short out-of-town trip. During her trip, Randy went down to the Halls' to help them out. Doyle asked Randy to help him into the next room. As he got up, he immediately collapsed in Randy's arms. He was gone.

Karyn returned home to the devastating news. She kicked their stove as she cried out, "He can't be gone. He had not accepted Jesus!"

It was a long night for Karyn as she felt the loss of her close friend and replayed all their conversations over the years, recalled all her prayers, all the progress made in Doyle's heart. She wanted to pray, but no words would come. Anger and fear welled up at the same time. Doyle's despondence the last time they were together haunted her now.

The next morning the phone rang. It was Beverly, Doyle's wife. She was a gruff woman and always got right to the point.

"Karyn, I got something to tell you that Doyle wanted you to know."

She went on to tell her that the night before Doyle died, he came out of the bedroom, asked her to find him a Bible, and said, "Bev, you need to help me receive Jesus into my heart."

She explained how they knelt down together and she read John 3:16, listening as Doyle received Jesus as his Lord and Savior. Doyle made Bev promise she would tell Karyn.

At this news, a joy beyond measure welled up within Karyn's spirit! Within the span of a few days, Karyn had gone from her lowest low to the highest high. She embraced Randy and tried to share the good news, but tears and emotion prevented her from conveying it until she was able to gather herself. Randy was struck by the news, an event he never believed would happen. They both wept tears of joy. Faith filled the Lee home that morning.

A few days later, Karyn and Randy went to the funeral home. Karyn could not help noticing the picture that was affixed to the open lid of Doyle's casket. It was identical to what she had seen in her dream, but with one exception: it was an empty field.

Karyn, filled with peace, whispered to Randy, "It's the same image as my dream, but no Doyle!"

Be joyful in hope, patient in affliction,
faithful in prayer. (Rom. 12:12)

6

Welcoming Jesus

The clouds ushered in the Lord of Hosts, and heaven exploded with exuberance. The Son had returned. He had conquered sin and death. The Son of God, scathed and scarred, yet restored. The perfect sacrifice. Away with the old order! Jesus is now the one and only High Priest through which humanity is granted direct access to the Father, his Father, through the Holy Spirit. This Spirit now resides freely within the hearts of all who believe.

The moment the Son returned—what must that moment have been like? Jesus's arrival into heaven's glory after a thirty-three-year absence is unimaginable.

He descended to earth to become one of God's prized creations—a human being. He wrapped himself in the same flesh as Adam and entered into the fallen world to restore it to its original glorious state. His great love for humanity propelled him to become human and to lay down his life for all humankind. He lowered himself and subjected himself to a suffering beyond comprehension, taking on and becoming sin.

And then came the separation from his Father, with whom he had been in unbroken fellowship throughout all eternity past. To be cut off and separated from his Father was an unfathomable sacrifice we cannot wrap our finite minds around. I was crushed emotionally when I was separated from my earthly father, whom I had known only an infinitesimal fraction of the time Jesus had known his Father. Christ's obedient sacrifice was a loving disruption that transforms the hearts of all who believe.

The moment had come. Jesus—the Son of God but also the Son of Man—was returning to God the Father, his Father. He was the same Jesus who had stepped out of glory, and yet he was forever different. Different in form and different in his understanding of humanity. He lowered himself to identify with all people, with a particular solidarity towards the lowly, the downcast, the rejected, the poor. He came to serve, not to be served (Matt. 20:28). He brought into glory, into the Trinity, an experiential, empathic understanding and deep love for the marginalized.

Jesus spoke his final words to the disciples just before his ascension. Surely he was sad to leave them, especially given the hard and challenging road he knew lay ahead for each of them. He would no longer be there in human form to explain situations, share stories, provide perfect examples and life lessons. His students were graduating, and they were headed out into the world to apply what they had been taught.

The students became the teachers as they watched Jesus ascend. This small handful of men, sold out to the cause and soon to be filled with the same Spirit as their Lord, would do even greater works than he had (John 14:12–14). But one must not forget, it was through his Spirit these works were accomplished.

Imagine how Jesus must have felt in those last few moments on earth as he anticipated the reunion just seconds away, as he was speaking his last physical words to them: "But you will receive power when the Holy Spirit comes on you; and you will be my witnesses in Jerusalem, and in all Judea and Samaria, and to the ends of the earth" (Acts 1:8). These words must have been so full of mystery to his disciples, who could not possibly have understood what this power would be like. Yet this was the way with so much of what Jesus taught; understanding was retrospective. Following Jesus always involves leaps of faith that only make sense over time.

With those last words spoken, he was now free to look up and allow the same Holy Spirit he just described to take him home. Jesus continued his work, preparing a place for them and for us. "My Father's house has many rooms; if that were not so, would I have told you that I am going there to prepare a place for you? And if I go and prepare a place for you, I will come back and take you to be with me that you also may be where I am" (John 14:2–3). As excited as Jesus was to return to heaven's glory in that moment, he also longed to return to his people, to come back so they could be together forever in the same place, body, soul, and spirit. While he looked forward to indwelling and empowering them through his Spirit, this was an incomplete "together." It was as incomplete as his own separation from his Father, for though he had the presence of the Spirit on earth, yet he was away from the Godhead. Jesus was already longing for the day when his followers, all of them, would be physically and spiritually present with him. Perhaps it's akin to writing, emailing, or texting a loved one as a way to connect, even though being with them in person is better by far.

Following Jesus always involves leaps of faith that only make sense over time.

> "Father, I want those you have given me to be with me where I am, and to see my glory, the glory you have given me because you loved me before the creation of the world." (John 17:24)

7

Divine Timing

I was nervous as I rang the doorbell. Jo opened the door and invited me in. I heard voices and laughter as we walked through the hall into the area where everyone was gathered. She introduced me to each of Dennis's family members—his son, daughter-in-law, and brother—and many of his friends. It was awkward to be in that space with people I didn't know, all of us putting on an air of normalcy when there was nothing normal about this time or space.

Across the room, the hospital bed had been rolled out onto the large deck overlooking the lake. I knew Dennis was in it, fighting for his life and losing the battle. I was there to see him, not to socialize, so I made my way out to the deck. Walking through the two large French doors Dennis had designed to bring the outside in, I was struck by how perfect this setup was for rolling his hospice bed out and letting him spend his last days in his favorite spot, overlooking Lake Macatawa. I was sure he hadn't foreseen that.

"Dennis, Mitch is here," Jo spoke softly in his ear.

Dennis heard her and exerted effort to move his head in affirmation.

"Wow, that's more than we've seen out of Dennis all day," Jo said with a smile. I was happy Dennis was still alert enough to know me, but at the same time I was deeply saddened by his sudden uncommunicative condition.

Three weeks earlier, I was in this same home celebrating with Dennis and his many friends. For years, Dennis and Jo hosted a Fourth of July celebration at their house on Pickle Bay, complete with music, food, drinks, and fireworks—some of their own and, visible from across the lake, some from the township's fireworks display. This party was special for me, as it was the first I had attended. I had often given Dennis grief for not putting me on his invite list, but this year was different. The coveted invitation had arrived, and I was thrilled to be there. It didn't matter that, in the back of my mind, I was pretty sure this was a reciprocal invite for my having invited Dennis to our design studio's ten-year anniversary celebration the year before. Memories of that night came to the forefront as I recalled Dennis standing up at dinner and toasting me, offering encouraging affirmations about the firm, my accomplishments, and our friendship, even his love for me.

At his Fourth of July party, it was clear Dennis had lost weight. He was visibly weak as he moved from guest to guest, greeting them and affirming, as was his way. He was fresh off some discouraging news about his prognosis. He had been given a year to live—but only if he went through the rigors of chemo. Without chemo, it was much shorter.

Death is so strange when it is staring you in the face through the eyes of a friend. He was excited to see me at the party. We embraced, and he whispered in my ear, "I told you I would invite you. I'm so glad you came!" We shared a moment in his backyard, and then he moved along, retreating to the house periodically to rest throughout the night.

Now my friend and design colleague had reached a point where it was all he could do to breathe. As I looked at Dennis in that bed, I was surprised at how quickly he had deteriorated and equally surprised I was able to be here during this time. Earlier that same day, as I was backing out of my driveway, I saw a neighbor across the street, a mutual friend of mine and Dennis's, and it prompted a strong feeling about Dennis. I knew Dennis was terminal, but he had a year or so to live, and I had just seen him a few weeks ago. But at that moment, I felt a sense of urgency well up within me. I called Jo that morning to check on him, and she welcomed me to stop by anytime.

I left work that evening intending to see Dennis and called my wife, Chris, on the way. She was heading to the beach to watch our son play volleyball, along with my sister-in-law and brother-in-law, who had just arrived from Atlanta. I told her I'd join them and just visit Dennis the next day, but she insisted I go see him right then, citing how much more important it was to see him at this time. As much as I wanted to avoid a difficult visit, I agreed and headed over to Dennis's home. I didn't know where Dennis was in his faith walk, as we were industry friends who knew and respected each other on a professional level but not necessarily a personal one.

Before I went in, I sent a group text to some of my work associates, asking for their prayers for Dennis and for an opportunity for me to pray with him. I received this beautiful prayer text in response from my colleague Jennifer:

> Lord God, you are the great healer of everything that
> is broken in this world. But your timing is not ours.
> We struggle to see suffering that seems so senseless
> when viewed through the clouded mirror that we
> have. I long for the day when I will see you and your
> works clearly and glorify you properly. Because you

ask us to come to you, I pray that you will bring a miracle into Dennis's life so he will have peace in the knowledge of Jesus. Make yourself crystal clear in these final hours, and if it be your will, heal his body, to your glory. Amen.

This prayer gave me comfort and peace as I stood next to the railing, Dennis behind me, looking out toward the lake. Why was I here at this time? I wanted to pray with Dennis, but how would that be possible with all these people around? No sooner had that thought crossed my mind than I turned to discover everyone had gone inside. I was alone on the deck with Dennis. So I approached him and asked if he would like me to pray with him. He nodded with a slight smile on his face. I do not recall the exact words I prayed, nor do I believe the words were mine alone, as they had the power of many others' prayers behind them. What I do recall was asking Jesus to come close, to wash away sin, to accept Dennis into his forever kingdom. I asked Dennis to look to Jesus and to look for Jesus. When I finished praying, there was a tear in his eye that had not been there before. That was my only sign that God had come close in that moment. In my remaining time with Dennis, I was able to affirm him, his life, his accomplishments, his family, and his legacy.

We struggle to see suffering that seems so senseless when viewed through the clouded mirror that we have.

Shortly after that, I left and joined my family out at the beach. Early the next morning, I received a text from Jo that Dennis had passed just after midnight. I was stunned. Stunned by the timing, stunned by God's providence, and stunned by the loss.

> "Where, O death, is your victory?
> Where, O death, is your sting?"

The sting of death is sin, and the power of sin
is the law. But thanks be to God! He gives us the
victory through our Lord Jesus Christ. Therefore,
my dear brothers and sisters, stand firm. Let
nothing move you. Always give yourselves fully to
the work of the Lord, because you know that your
labor in the Lord is not in vain. (1 Cor. 15:55–58)

8

The Unimaginable Happening

It was early evening on Thursday, August 15, 1996. Chris was at the grocery store, and I was home with our three boys. The boys were all engaged in either homework or games. I had a quiet moment and felt prompted to call my sister Karyn.

I was caught off guard when a man with an unfamiliar voice answered. Initially I thought I had misdialed. "I'm sorry. I must have the wrong number. I was dialing the Lee residence."

"This is the Lee residence."

Now I was really confused, not to mention concerned.

"Is Karyn there?"

"Yes, but she is unable to speak right now."

"I'm her brother," I said rather forcefully. "Who are you?"

"I'm her pastor," he said after a very long pause. "Branden is dead."

Branden . . . my nephew . . . *dead?*

I don't have any recollection of the rest of that conversation, other than it was short. My mind was racing, while panic, fear, profound sadness, and utter confusion hit me all at once. I knew I needed to go to Karyn right away. This was before cell phones existed, so I was not able to quickly reach Chris. The wait for her to return home seemed endless. I felt like a caged animal. I was so anxious to get on the road, anxious to break the news to Chris, anxious to be with Karyn and Randy, and just anxious in general.

Chris finally pulled up. I met her in the garage and blurted out, "Branden died. We need to leave now!" She was stunned, and details were few. We only knew that the unthinkable, the unimaginable, and the worst nightmare for any parent and for any family had happened to Karyn and Randy and their daughter Shawna. The darkness of death loomed over us all. The ripple effect of his passing would span years and decades.

We dealt with the groceries, pulled together suitcases and duffle bags, told our boys, David, Josh, and Seth, what had happened. We immediately left Green Bay, Wisconsin, and drove most of the night around Michigan's upper peninsula, across the Mackinac Bridge, and down to their home in South Boardman.

Death is as mysterious as it is painful, but the death of a child is beyond, so far beyond, our ability to comprehend. This was senseless, random, tragic, life-altering, and awful on every level. My nephew, a wonderful thirteen-year-old boy, his entire life ahead of him. How was this possible? How could he be gone so early, so suddenly? A tragic accident took him from us and left us swirling in confusion and grief.

We finally pulled into their driveway. They lived in a baby-blue farmhouse with a wraparound porch, perched on a hill surrounded by sixty acres of farmland and woods. Memories flooded through my mind of all the time spent at this idyllic place with this amazing family—my family—a family in shock, a family wrecked by a sudden and senseless loss. I reflected on how much a part of me was a part of them: from their wedding day to the day

I held Shawna in my arms as a five-day-old infant; the day I first held Branden; all the ensuing years that unfolded in their small town, on their property, and in and around their refurbished, old farmhouse; the family that grew up there, the memories built there, the smiles and laughter, the stories told, the stories written, the pure magic that was the Lee family.

I ran from the car into the house. I went straight upstairs where I heard voices. Karyn fell into my arms. I sat on the edge of the bed holding her. We wept and sat in silence for what seemed like forever. Words are useless in the depth of tragedy. Just being there is all one can do. It's both the most and the least one can do. In reality, we can offer nothing, do nothing. Helpless, we can only be present in the face of such a great loss.

> *At times, the unimaginable happens, and it simply defies logic or explanation. Like Job in the Old Testament, we can only sit amidst the wreckage and exist.*

We want to believe the Lord is watching over us, and I know he is. We want to believe God is sovereign and in control of every circumstance. We want to believe tragedy strikes others, not us. I have learned, however, that tragedy is no respecter of persons. At times, the unimaginable happens, and it simply defies logic or explanation. Like Job in the Old Testament, we can only sit amidst the wreckage and exist, the heavy weight of sorrow pressing in from every side, so crushing and overpowering we can hardly bear it.

He was such a sweet child. He enjoyed drawing and fishing. Recently, I was admiring some of his artwork that had been framed and positioned prominently on the walls of Karyn's home. I, too, had drawn as a child, so I could relate to his love for art and, through it, his storytelling. A pencil and a blank sheet of paper was all he needed to lose himself within the lines on the page. So much of his art had biblical themes: Jesus's sacrifice on the cross, praying in the garden, battling the enemy of our souls. Jesus was often the subject; I loved how much Branden loved

Jesus. He was so sensitive to his surroundings and spiritually attuned at such a young age.

Twenty-two years have passed since Branden was welcomed into the arms of his Savior. He left a hole in our hearts that won't be filled until we meet again around the throne.

9

An Unimaginable Grief

During the early days of deep grief, Karyn and Randy would walk, and walk, and walk. One morning, Karyn walked alone. It was a cold, rainy fall morning. As was her routine, she was walking with her head down and buried under her hood, staring at the wet pavement with each step. She was desperately broken and second-guessing her faith. How could heaven be so silent, and where was the confirmation that Branden is okay? She reflected on Branden and his close bond with his Papa (our father, Karl). Branden had taken Papa's death four years earlier so hard. She recalled Branden's words after Papa's funeral: "Mom, how can I bring people to Christ at my funeral, like Papa did?"

Just then, as she was walking, my sister found herself covered in sunshine, the land around her transformed into an otherworldly state, unspeakably beautiful. The heavy burden she was carrying vanished as joyous contentment enveloped her. She noticed Branden at her side with Yogi, their family dog, between them. Yogi was Branden's first dog, who had passed away years earlier. She reached over to pet Yogi and noticed Branden's hand on Yogi as well. In this state of comfort, joy, and love, Karyn found herself full of joy and laughter. Looking up, she saw Karl coming toward them. As he came closer, she could see his eyes were fixed on Branden. His smile warm and inviting, he approached with arms wide open and moved into a glorious embrace of his grandson.

As suddenly as the vision had begun, it ended. Karyn was back in the real world—or rather, the earthly world. Back into the cold, the rain, and the pain. The heavy burdens that had momentarily lifted settled back over her. Yet in this unimaginable vision, God, in his divine mercy, had given her a glimpse of heaven, a glimpse into the eternal, where Karl and Branden resided together. It was an unexpected gift of comfort and a window opening out onto her future hope in glory. The vision changed everything for her, not by making her present reality any less painful but by giving her a picture of a hope-filled future and by renewing her endurance. It was the foreshadowing of a pain-free, relationship-rich, eternal dwelling with her loved ones. "Blessed are those who mourn, for they will be comforted" (Matt. 5:4).

For a long period after Branden's passing, Karyn was not able to communicate with the outside world, not even her siblings. Standing on the outside looking in, we understood, but it felt like a double loss at times. Living so many miles away, the hole in my heart grew larger and larger. I longed for normalcy, for a return to that place in time that could never again be. This was a time of complete silence between us. Not a call, a note, or an email was returned. I could only pray and wonder what kind of pain she was going through. Prayer was all I had, and even that was difficult as I struggled against the bitterness and anger toward God that had crept in.

One afternoon I sat in front of my computer and penned

these words, which made their way into a frame, then a FedEx box, and eventually onto my sister's porch:

A CELEBRATION OF LIFE

Branden's life, may it forever be a testimony
      of God's glorious grace to us.
May his gentle presence, humor, and warmth,
his sensitivity and compassion be present with
      us always.
He was big and strong yet equally gentle and meek.
He was growing up and on the brink of manhood,
yet he longed to be forever young.
His eternal youth is heaven's gain.
He appreciated the little things in life
and was sensitive to the feelings of others,
never wanting harm or hurt to come to anyone.
He shared a special relationship with his mother.
The times when she needed it, his comfort and
      warmth were there.
He knew, even when others didn't . . . he knew.
May the memories of that special bond fill your
      heart always.
He left his art, which gently points us to the Savior
      who can be trusted with our whys.
May grief subside, giving way to a peaceful joy
      as we celebrate Branden's life.
And may his life be as alive in our hearts as it is
      in his new heavenly home.

To the best of my ability, I sought to capture and celebrate Branden's life in this poem by taking an honest look at his short, beautiful time on earth through the eyes of faith, eternity, and our faithful Savior. I also hoped these words would be a way of connecting, of offering some healing, perhaps even restoring our relationship, which had been torn apart by grief alone. For weeks I waited, but no response came.

Then one day, a call. It was Karyn. The box had been placed by their back door, which was seldom used. So it had gone unnoticed until, in the dead of winter, Randy spotted its cardboard edge peeking up through a snowdrift. A welcome surprise, she said. It had warmed them on a particularly icy-cold day.

Tragedy is an unwelcome beast that must be ridden and tamed. During the ride, one is convinced they will be bucked off and destroyed, and yet there is no choice but to ride, to hang on and endure the rough, painful, crushing blows.

Hearing her voice over the phone—her gratitude, her love—melted my heart. My lost sister was speaking again, reaching out, reconnecting.

Tragedy is an unwelcome beast that must be ridden and tamed. During the ride, one is convinced they will be bucked off and destroyed, and yet there is no choice but to ride, to hang on and endure the rough, painful, crushing blows. It may have taken years, but with divine courage and strength, the Lee family (and our family) made it through the worst darkness until hope shone through. We won't be the same, and an ache in our hearts will always be there, but the presence of a future hope makes the ache bearable.

Set Free

"Set Free" is an allegory inspired by a Tim Keller message.

How I ended up here is beyond me. Immersed in a damp and lonely place where the sun rarely shone, I had the essentials for survival, but this was no way to live. I had only a fragment of my own will in this place. The things I longed to do, I couldn't do. That which I absolutely didn't want to do, I was dragged away and forced to do.

Day after day, I was awakened in the early morning hours by the sound of the guards dragging their billy clubs along the bars of our cells. Within moments, we were required to stand at attention while our doors unlocked, and then we were ushered out into the yard. The only solace I found in this place was in the companionship of the men who stood with me. We were forbidden to speak to each other when the guards were present, but we knew each other well from our many conversations between our cell walls at night. I was grateful for my cell mates. If it were not for them, I would have given up. Who could endure this treatment alone?

The guards were cruel in every way. Occasionally I would catch a glimpse of their eyes as the sentries lorded over us, strolling back and forth in a show of their dominance. It was like staring into an abyss, completely void of anything resembling kindness, love, or care. Our pain was their pleasure, soullessly inventing new ways to torture us, it seemed they would go to any lengths to eliminate whatever hope, dignity, or humanity that remained. A tactic they sometimes used was to offer a tiny glimmer of hope, a sliver of light, a chance to improve our circumstances, only to rip it away and reveal it as a mirage. Raising our hopes only to further crush them was a source of sick, demented pleasure for them.

Over time, I became full of hate. I hated my circumstances. I hated that I had no will of my own. I hated my torturers. And I hated myself. My world became darker with each passing day. My will to go on without any answers, barely able even to recall my questions, was mystifying to me. Hate had stripped everything away, down to a valueless existence.

My despair was the goal of my oppressors, and I knew it. What I hated most of all was I had succumbed, had become like them: hate-filled beings without a shred of hope. Deep within, I knew this was not who I was, but I had no clue how to change. The one thing, perhaps the only thing I knew for sure was any change within me would not come from within me. It would have to come from outside of me.

Shortly after this realization, a breakthrough occurred. It started with an unusual sound coming from the cell next to me. It was the sound of hope. Was it laughter? Joy? Perhaps singing?

I pressed against the wall and whispered loudly, "What's going on?"

A loud whisper came back, "Haven't you heard?"

"Heard what?"

"The war is over! We are free."

I had to let that sink in. I wasn't sure if the news was reliable or if it could possibly be true. But a flicker of hope sparked within me.

The next morning was just like all the others as the familiar rattling of the billy clubs against the bars roused me from sleep. We were ushered into the yard. Nothing had practically changed in my situation, but as tiny as it was, the seed of hope was enough to melt away a thin layer of my hatefulness, enough to shift my perspective. I began to see things differently, yet remained cautious. Was this just another one of the many tricks the guards were playing on us? A false hope intended to crush our spirits again?

Days passed, one after another after another. Nothing changed externally, but internally, positive change was happening as I opened myself more and more to the anticipation of victory. The official news hadn't yet reached our camp, and the guards were oblivious, still treating us in the same torturous way. Nothing had changed and yet everything had changed at the same time.

I also knew who I was: a child of the King, part of an army that holds up the banner of victory over evil, injustice, and hatred.

The guards now seemed so very far away. I knew their days were numbered. At any moment, our army was going to appear over the eastern hill to capture our enemy and set us free at last.

I knew who I wasn't: no longer a helpless captive, enslaved by an evil master.

I also knew who I was: a child of the King, part of an army that holds up the banner of victory over evil, injustice, and hatred.

> For our struggle is not against flesh and
> blood, but against the rulers, against the
> authorities, against the powers of this dark

world and against the spiritual forces of
evil in the heavenly realms. (Eph. 6:12)

But if Christ is in you, then even though your
body is subject to death because of sin, the Spirit
gives life because of righteousness. And if the
Spirit of him who raised Jesus from the dead is
living in you, he who raised Christ from the dead
will also give life to your mortal bodies because
of his Spirit who lives in you. (Rom. 8:10–11)

11

Pivot to Christ

Fresh off of high school graduation, I was looking forward to college, a career, and adult life. Although if I'm honest, it would be a stretch to say that I truly was "looking forward" to what lay ahead. High school, for me, was about living in the moment. It was about enjoying life and living as if it would never come to an end.

I especially enjoyed sports. My years on the football field and my time on the ice playing hockey were exhilarating—the love of the game, the thrill of scoring and sometimes winning but also learning to lose. We had plenty of practice losing. Of course, the thrill of winning and celebrating was the best, but learning how to handle injustice and unfairness, even in my early days of sports, was something I carried forward and applied to adulthood. Experiencing "team" by learning how to rely on others, to lead, and to put individual desires aside for group goals, created a rapport and a bond that somehow made the long hours of practice and sacrifice worth it. But while it's true I developed many valuable lifelong skills on the athletic field, there was a much deeper need for growth that I had yet to address.

Experiences in fringe charismatic churches during my grade school and middle school years left me disillusioned as I tried to make sense of the hypocrisy I witnessed. My own parents oscillated from being spiritually passionate to being spiritually tepid and eventually succumbed to cold disillusionment. By the time I entered high school, my family had settled back into a formal, structured church setting but seemed to have written off Christianity as a charade. I kept attending Sunday services with them throughout high school, but by then I had left the God of my childhood. I had witnessed enough, both internally and externally, to know that God was real, but I decided I didn't want anything to do with him. Unfortunately and unwittingly, I had formed my views of God through the observational lens of humans. Therefore, the agnostic lifestyle suited me just fine. I lived my high school years in a throw-caution-to-the-wind manner. To this day, I have regrets for some decisions I made during those years as well as decisions I didn't make. Perhaps none of my actions were indictable, but it's not hard to imagine the lifestyle of a teenage boy with popularity, charisma, and good looks. I capitalized on my charm for personal gain. The cliché "high school dream" was my reality, and I didn't feel bad about it in the least.

But everything changed on a Saturday night in the middle of July 1979. Only a handful of my friends were still at the party I was hosting in my home (technically my parents' home, and they were out of town). The conversation with my friends that night turned spiritual, not because of some religious intention but because of a movie that had been released the previous year that was still receiving a lot of attention. The film, *Damien: Omen 2*, was a sequel to *The Omen*. It was a horror flick really, with Antichrist themes and a demonic plot. We had fun discussing the movie and querying each other about our positions on the spirit world. Questions came up about Satan and the demonic realm and whether we believed in such things. At some point in the discussion, over a can of beer, I had a cool idea.

"Hey, my folks have a tape of a live deliverance. Do you want me to see if I can find it?"

I received an enthusiastic response, so I raced upstairs and rifled through my parents' box of audio cassette tapes from our early charismatic days.

"I found it!" I exclaimed, running down the stairs, anxious to play it for its entertainment value.

The room became silent as we all listened intently to this cassette tape of a live deliverance recorded in the 1960s in Atlanta. The recording captured the deliverance of Jane, a mother who was under tremendous attack. Her condition had deteriorated to the point that her husband planned to institutionalize her for the sake and safety of their children. In a last-ditch effort, he called a Baptist minister and his elders to cast nineteen demons out of Jane. It was eerie to listen to this woman scream and then speak, or more accurately, the demons speak through her, to these men. Each demon displayed a different personality, but they all had the same goal: to destroy this woman's life and the lives of her children.

This tape is what God used to wake me up along with a few others at my home on that summer night almost forty years ago now. I'll never forget how he spoke to me that night. The messages were clear.

I am real.

The enemy is real.

Life is not a game.

Repent.

Receive me as your Lord and Savior now.

Those messages came rushing through me as I found myself on my knees along with a few close friends. At eighteen, I was ready to turn from my sin and receive him. This was not just a prayer. Those moments of decision were lifelong, and I knew it. I knew Jesus was not asking me to receive him into my heart as a safety net to protect me from hell. No. He was clear. And it was clear that he was asking for all of me (a genuine conversion). He was inviting me to be born again, which required a death, the death of myself.

That night I stayed up most of the night. I couldn't sleep. I spent time reading the Bible. For some reason I read through the book of Revelation. Perhaps this was linked to God revealing himself to me. The words came alive. I had read my Bible before, but it was always boring, forced, and anything but alive. Yet now this book came mysteriously alive to me, not only that night but day after day following my conversion. Discovering Jesus was called "the Word" and he was inseparable from the words in the Bible helped me to understand the power of the Holy Spirit to be a tangible, accessible presence in my life. God used a conversation about a horror film among teenagers to shine his light into our darkness.

As I look back over the years of my life, I am still amazed by the clarity of those moments and how transformative the decision was that night. It altered the course of my life right up to this moment as I am typing these words.

I was ready, ashamed that I had abandoned my faith and walked away from the God of my youth. I felt Jesus come close that night in a way I hadn't experienced before. I felt the cleansing power of repentance along with the newness and power of his Spirit now resident within me. I knew, for the first time, that I was his. Later, I would read, "The Spirit himself testifies with our spirit that we are God's children" (Rom. 8:16).

The hand of God is as mysterious as it is magnificent.

My high school years were no doubt a time of exploration and growing up, but on my own terms. I'm so thankful that God has a way, a supernatural way of drawing us toward truth and using whatever context we find ourselves in to bring understanding of the fullness of the gospel of Jesus Christ. My experience in sports—learning to play on and function as a team—allowed me to see so many common themes with the way the church functions in the world. It's comprised of individuals with varying gifts and abilities, all working together for the common goal of advancing the kingdom and ultimately winning the prize.

Pivoting to Christ in acceptance was just the beginning of my heart change, and while for me it was a rather abrupt change, for many it is more gradual. Everything was different for me: my perspective on life, my decisions, how I used my time, even the thoughts I entertained. A commitment to studying the Bible was critical to my faith walk, because the Bible contains the very words of God, and his Spirit brings those words to life for all who believe and are willing to put their belief into action. I knew lasting change would require community, which led me to join a church. Shortly after being publicly baptized, I engaged with a handful of new friends who took their faith seriously, prayed for me, and held me accountable.

> *One must never forget it is a battle, progress takes faith, and faith is intentional and not without effort and choice.*

The faith walk is long and filled with many challenges. One must never forget it is a battle, progress takes faith, and faith is intentional and not without effort and choice. Many times I have wandered, and other times I have wondered where God is. Yet he has always been faithful, even when I have not. I'm thankful I am still pursuing him and he has never stopped pursuing me.

The Word became flesh and made his
dwelling among us. We have seen his glory, the
glory of the one and only Son, who came from
the Father, full of grace and truth. (John 1:14)

12

Life Is but a Dream

We need to take dreams more literally
and waking life more symbolically.
–ROBERT MOSS–

There are three states to every human experience: a conscious physical state, a resting sleep state (where dreams reside), and a future eternal state on the other side of this life. Our lives could be analogous to a dream, for a day is coming when believers will awaken to a reality beyond our most vivid imaginings. Paul directs us in this when he writes in 2 Corinthians 4:18, "So we fix our eyes not on what is seen, but on what is unseen, since what is seen is temporary, but what is unseen is eternal."

Paul is referring to the spiritual realm when he says we fix our eyes on the unseen. In his earlier letter to the Corinthian church, he describes our poor range of spiritual vision: "For now we see in a mirror dimly, but then face to face. Now I know in part; then I shall know fully, even as I have been fully known" (1 Cor. 13:12 ESV).

What additional insight emerges if we overlay these two verses?

> So we fix our eyes not on what is seen, but on what is unseen, like seeing in a mirror dimly, since what is seen is temporary, but what is unseen is eternal and can only be partially known.

Or in more contemporary language:

> Gaze intently at the invisible, which is unclear and blurry, keeping in mind that all you can see is impermanent and what you cannot see or fully know is permanent and everlasting.

It's easy to pass over these verses quickly because initially they make perfect sense, right? Focus on God and heaven, the permanent, and not on earthly things that are fading away, the temporary. But when the two verses are combined, we see the challenge in living this way. These verses describe two vastly different worlds, which operate simultaneously: the one we live in now and the one we will live in later but exists now as well.

We should view this earthly experience as temporary and our eternal spiritual state as permanent. Our earthly reality, our "now" state, is in clear focus each day, easy to see. It is the only reality we have fully experienced. Believers in Jesus understand our earthly, temporary state to be a fading reality, one that is not our guiding focus. We are drawn toward a focus on the cosmic, permanent reality, the enduring spiritual world. This unseen world is so great that even a fuzzy view or incomplete knowledge of it is enough to sustain us until we arrive home. First Corinthians 2:9–10 gives us a stunning vision of what is to come: "'What no eye has seen, what no ear has heard, and what no human mind has conceived'—the things God has prepared for those who love him—these are the things God has revealed to us by his Spirit."

Perhaps our awake, conscious state is akin to our sleep state when we have dreams that seem completely real but that we immediately dismiss as fantasy when we awaken. Now suppose you don't awaken and you stay in the dream; that fantasy dream state would become your reality, and you might come to see it as your only reality. Meanwhile, the fully-awake, real world continues to operate outside your consciousness as you slumber, even though you are unaware.

We have all had dreams that we thought were real, and no one in our dreams would have been able to convince us otherwise. Paul is awakening us to the cosmic, permanent reality that lies outside of this life. It's as if he's saying, "Fix your eyes not on what you are seeing in this dream; rather, fix them on the future state you cannot see but will see when you awaken."

There is more beyond the world we live in today—an unseen spiritual reality unfolding now and throughout eternity. If we consider again the two passages from Paul's letters to the Corinthians, melded into one and seen through this dream-state lens, something like this emerges:

> We fix our eyes not on what we see in this dream; rather, we fix our eyes on the real world where we will be awake and alive in an unimaginable way. While we can't fully grasp the extent of the real yet unseen world, we can humbly accept that we see through a glass dimly.

Much like describing the Grand Canyon to someone who has not seen it with their own eyes, words don't do it justice, but the listener is able to imagine its grandeur. And in so doing, they begin to look forward with great anticipation to seeing that which cannot be adequately described.

It is hard to imagine that our present reality will be gone and replaced with a new, permanent, eternal state. This is often the opposite of our current thinking—that our physical state is real and permanent, while our future spiritual state is more of a dream and somewhat unreal.

A friend of mine, David, recently shared an experience he had with his young son. They were together in an amusement park, and his son was having a fantasy experience on a ride with a virtual reality (VR) headset on. David stood next to him while his son was engaging with an imaginary world. In this cool, dark room, David watched him reach for things that didn't exist and react to the unreal as if it were real. At a certain point in the experience, his son became fearful and yelled out, "Daddy, are you here?" David reach out and touched his son on the shoulder saying, "Yes, Daddy is right here." To me, this captures the essence of what Paul was conveying. Don't get so caught up in this VR life. Your heavenly Father lives outside of it yet is near you on this earthly ride. And while you cannot remove the VR headset (yet), know that he is with you. Your future "real" state lies just outside and ahead of you now. Keep your focus on that reality; keep your focus on him.

You can start now, living with the eternal perspective of the unseen world. Begin by fixing your eyes on the spiritual world that is exceedingly more real than the current, temporary world.

Wake up and restore your spiritual sight! You can start now, living with the eternal perspective of the unseen world. Begin by fixing your eyes on the spiritual world that is exceedingly more real than the current, temporary world. Start living outside your dream. Don't believe the lie that tells you to live *for the dream*. Be less consumed by the temporary and more consumed by the permanent. Start living for the hidden, eternal world today.

13

My Selfish Life

There are only a few times in my life when I can say I felt as if time stood still, and this was one of those times. We were turning right onto Benjamin Avenue when I heard those life-altering words: "I'm pregnant!" Even now, some forty years removed from that time and space, I can still transport myself back into that white Pontiac sedan where those words were blurted out by my girlfriend, Ann. Her words reverberated in my head along with all the repercussions they would have for my life.

My life. My life was all I cared about in that moment. I was scared, and my immediate response was self-preservation. I was unable or unwilling to consider anyone else, not even the child—my child—that was rapidly growing, hidden away yet openly visible to God. My mind raced, but first toward what all this meant for *my* life. I was only seventeen; I thrived on my freedom, popularity, and dreams for the future. Would college now be out of the question? Would I be obliged to marry young? I imagined the public shame and embarrassment and how I would tell my father, who had sternly warned me about this and whose wrath I feared more than anything else on the planet.

So often in our youth we live as if consequences don't exist, until they do.

Blinded by selfishness, I set off to research my options, thinking only about how to fix the situation for myself. The year was 1977, four years since the landmark *Roe v. Wade* decision that legalized abortions without parental consent. I'll never forget my phone conversation with the woman at the abortion clinic. She was so kind and reassuring as she walked me through the simple process of aborting this pregnancy. It was like I had gotten into a fender bender and my insurance agent was walking me through the process of repairing a damaged quarter panel that would make everything as good as new. She helped abate my fear and anxiety. All the consequences I was obsessing over would simply go away. All that was left was to convince Ann this was our only logical option. Alas, she didn't share my perspective. In fact, she was considering having this child.

To my shame, in time, I was able to wear her down. She reluctantly went ahead with my wishes, perhaps because they were a strong signal I was not interested in her or in being connected to her for the remainder of my life. I don't really know. I only felt relief when it was over, remorse would come later, much later. I wanted to be there for her and take her to the surgery, but she went alone without a mention of it to me until it was over. Perhaps I hadn't earned that right, perhaps she had picked up on my caring only that it went away. Which it did. That is, until it didn't.

Seven years after the abortion, I had my college degree in furniture design and was fostering a budding career in West Michigan. I was single and living alone in my own apartment. On this particular weekday morning, I woke to what I thought was a dream of a child crying. To my surprise, the crying didn't go away as I moved around the apartment and prepared for my day. I remember a sense of knowing, almost immediately, that this cry was the cry of my child. I felt it to my core.

I arrived at work and got busy painting the photo studio in our plant. It was quiet and I was alone, except for the sound of the crying child, an unceasing cry all morning long. When lunchtime came, I was more than ready to leave my quiet surroundings to run out and grab a bite, in hopes that the crying would subside. On my way out, I grabbed my Bible from my desk and headed off to Mr. Burger. As I sat in the booth, I prayed, "Lord, if this is your hand, reveal yourself to me." I wasn't sure what was happening, and I definitely was not prepared for what happened next. I took my Bible, opened it randomly, put my finger down on a verse, and began to read.

> For you created my inmost being; you knit me together in my mother's womb. I praise you because I am fearfully and wonderfully made; your works are wonderful, I know that full well. My frame was not hidden from you when I was made in the secret place, when I was woven together in the depths of the earth. Your eyes saw my unformed body; all the days ordained for me were written in your book before one of them came to be. (Ps. 139:13–16)

I closed my Bible, stunned—the hand of God had so overtly answered my prayer to reveal himself. I sat and reflected on how the child I had silenced and hidden from the world was now revealing himself or herself to me, first through a cry and now through words.

You might think an event like this would awaken me and cause me to come out from the shadow of this secret. After all, I had encountered the supernatural. But I didn't know what to do with this experience. To be honest, I was still afraid, still wanting it to go away. I told myself this was just between me and God. So I kept my secret safely tucked away and moved forward with my life. Things progressed predictably: marriage, children, home ownership. Years passed without any more supernatural interruptions or disruptions, and my secret remained tucked away, even from my wife, Chris. Events like the births of our children caused me to secretly reflect, but I quickly ushered those thoughts away. Perhaps God's revelation to me in 1984 at Mr. Burger was his way of revealing my sin and allowing me to own it; perhaps it was the end of the story, but I suspected not.

> I had encountered the supernatural. But I didn't know what to do with this experience. To be honest, I was still afraid, still wanting it to go away.

14

Life, Grace, and Healing

On Saturday evening, January 20, 1995, I sat in a chair in the living room of our home in Rockford, Michigan. My good friend Kevin Rubly was reclining on the floor in front of me, and, as was the case for many of our talks, this one had extended into the late hours. I remember glancing at my watch. It was just past midnight and officially Sunday when I felt compelled to share my hidden story with Kevin. I spoke quietly.

I was finishing the story and was up to the part where I went out for lunch and opened my Bible. For effect, I reached over and grabbed my Bible and said, "Kevin, I sat there in that booth at Mr. Burger, opened my Bible"—I randomly spread the pages and dropped my finger—"and put my finger right on Psalm 139:13." I looked down to find my finger on the very same verse. I looked up at Kevin, he looked back at me, and neither of us knew what to say except, "Wow." I had finally shared my secret with someone; unloading it was cathartic.

Kevin left and I went off to bed. Later that morning, Chris

and I discovered our second son, Josh, was sick. Chris had an obligation at church, so we agreed I would stay home with him. Before Chris headed out the door, she turned on our kids' cassette player to comfort Josh. The song that happened to be playing was Psalm 139:13–16 put to music. Coincidence? I think not. Chris arrived back home a few hours later. She walked in the house and immediately asked if I knew what day it was. I said no, and she replied, "It's National Right to Life Day." Of course it was.

As if that weren't enough, Chris informed me the library book I had inquired about weeks earlier was in, and she had picked it up for me: *Tilly,* written by Frank Peretti. It was a realistic fiction book about a girl who was aborted and was speaking in first-person narrative from her place in heaven. It was a painful story but laced with grace and forgiveness. Sunday evening rolled around, and I decided to head down to church to hear the woman Chris had heard speak that morning and who was speaking again tonight. She was the director of the Women's Center in Grand Rapids, which works with expectant moms to assist them in keeping their babies and choosing life. I can't recall her message, but I made my way up to her after the service to introduce myself and ask if she would be willing to meet with me sometime.

The very next morning, I sat across the desk from her and told her my story. To my surprise, she was not taken aback by it. I had assumed she would be struck by the supernatural elements, but she wasn't, which perhaps was an indication this type of story was familiar to her. She was much more interested in my completing the process of healing and restoration than my story. Most likely, she said, I was dealing with post-abortion trauma, which I found hard to believe given that nineteen years had passed. But I heard her out.

She proceeded to list the next steps I needed to take, the first of which was to tell my wife, and the second, to find Ann and apologize to her in person. If she had given me an alternative choice to climb Mount Everest, I would have chosen that over what she was suggesting. I had hidden this for so long from so many, and now the time had come—and was long overdue actually—for me to face the consequences head-on.

I decided to tell Chris after her night shift at the hospital. I was sitting at the kitchen table and simply said, "We need to talk." She fell silent and looked at me with an uneasy fear; I know her mind was racing with a thousand what-ifs. I began to share the story from the very beginning and only made it halfway before I began to weep. I was so sorry on so many levels—sorry I had allowed this to happen, sorry I had hidden it, sorry I had chosen to end a life. Sorry, sorry, sorry. As I wept, she gently put her hands on my shoulders and let me know she forgave me. We cried together that night. The healing had finally begun.

As time passed, we knew we would be okay. Our marriage would survive, and I was experiencing forgiveness through the eyes of my wife. To this day, Chris works with teen moms, helping those who choose life in the face of awful and painful circumstances. Each one of those girls is a hero to me, as is Chris for dedicating her life to these young women.

It took me some time, but eventually I was able to track down Ann. She was living in northern Michigan and was going through a divorce. She was very confused by my request to meet but obliged. It was midmorning, I was nervous as I pressed the doorbell. Ann opened the door and invited me in. I sensed her desire to get this over with posthaste. She directed me down the hall and we sat on a dark sofa in a room just off the kitchen. Our time together was somewhat uneventful. I made my apology as a tangible coldness hung around us. I left shortly after I had arrived, feeling I had gone through the motions just to say I did it.

But I know God had ordained that time, and my apology was an important part of my own healing—and Ann's too, I pray.

I thought this was the end of my process and that God had

brought me through to the other side where I was ready to receive his forgiveness and grace. It was a sunny day several months after my apology to Ann. Driving down the road, I was suddenly hit with a wave of grief like none I had experienced before. I wept to the point I could not drive, so I pulled over to the side of the road and cried uncontrollably. In that moment, I was given the revelation I was weeping for my child. And then God spoke to me, not in an audible voice, but in my heart: "Feel what I felt. Grieve like I grieved when you ended this life." Those words—words I will never forget—sunk deep into me that afternoon. They have reverberated throughout my life for twenty-two years now. For I know how much my God cares, how much he grieves for the helpless and hurting, including a tiny unborn child whose life was prematurely extinguished.

> God cares about our restoration and closure. He patiently walks alongside us, slowly revealing the path that leads his children into healing, for us and for those whom we have injured.

He cares deeply, and at times he calls us into those depths with him, to feel the pain and to move toward others who are in pain, offering grace, love, and forgiveness. Offering us restoration.

While I have lived into forgiveness and grace, regret and sorrow will never be fully expunged from my experience. Forgiveness won't fully erase the effects of sinful choices. Jesus's scars, the effect of our sin, will always be with him and a visible reminder.

My story (this story) is a demonstration of how much God cares about our restoration and closure. He patiently walks alongside us, slowly revealing the path that leads his children into healing, for us and for those whom we have injured. He desires for us to own our part as well as offer complete forgiveness to all who have sinned against us—without this, restoration won't occur.

> Strive for full restoration, encourage one another,
> be of one mind, live in peace. And the God of
> love and peace will be with you. (2 Cor. 13:11)

15

Without a Doubt

To say I was anxious was an understatement. We had known each other for nearly four years. Chris was my best friend, the one I had fallen in love with. She was eighteen when we met between services in a hallway at Calvary Undenominational Church. It wasn't my home church. In fact, I was only there because a good friend of mine, Ken, asked if I would go with him to check it out. We went to their young-adult Sunday school class and were making our way to the sanctuary when two young women, Chris and Shelly, introduced themselves to us. This sounds crazy, but Ken married Shelly and I married Chris. I knew Chris was the one for me. She was grounded in her faith, was a natural leader, and came from an amazing family. We had an organic chemistry and attraction to each other that grew slowly into a deep connection and love.

The saying, "Don't marry the person you can live with; marry the person you can't live without," applied to Chris's being for me without a doubt. Despite all the ways I knew she was right for me, my anxiety during our engagement was palpable. We knew each other so well, and fortunately for me, Chris knew my worries were not an indication of a lack of love for her. I didn't want to be hesitant, especially during what, for most couples, was a joyous time of celebration. I longed for that deep contentment as we planned our wedding, our honeymoon, our future home, and everything that lay ahead for us. Our engagement was a short three months, by design not necessity. It was not, however, an easy three months for me, and I found myself trusting God like never before. It would have been helpful if I could have identified the root cause of my hesitancy, but I couldn't. Even looking back now, it's pure speculation . . . my melancholy temperament, the fear of being tied down, my tendency to overthink big decisions, not being deserving of her, all the above?

My situation was akin to when a pilot, flying in a storm, has the sensation the plane is upside down and heading in the wrong direction. But upon looking down at the instruments, he realizes that the plane is upright and on course. Pilots must learn to trust their instruments over their feelings. I needed to do the same. Even though I wanted to pull back and pull out, when I considered all the facts, I knew I was heading in the right direction. Because I desired to be at peace, I sought out supernatural confirmations— which God is certainly not required to provide, and yet at times he does. In my case he provided three.

The first came on a Saturday. I was reading a best-selling book by Ed Wheat titled *Intended for Pleasure*, and a comment he made in one of the chapters caught my attention. If you have any doubts during your engagement, he said, don't go through with it. As you might imagine, this spun me big-time. It was 1986, so technology was pretty limited—no internet, no cell phones, no email. I looked on the back jacket of the book and saw that the author's medical practice was in Little Rock, Arkansas. So I picked up the phone, dialed information, and asked to be put through to his office. I anticipated voicemail; instead, a man picked up.

"Hello, is Dr. Ed Wheat available?" I inquired.

"Who is this?" the man replied.

"This is Mitch. I was reading Dr. Wheat's book, and I read something very disturbing regarding calling off your engagement if you have any doubts."

At that, the voice on the other end confessed, "I'm Dr. Ed Wheat. I don't usually answer the phone, especially on weekends. You caught me off guard."

He then went into diagnostic doctor mode, asking lots of questions about our relationship and background. After my discourse, he blurted out, "It sounds like *you* have the problem, young man. It has nothing to do with Chris!" He then encouraged me, recommended that I stay the course, and prayed with me. This all seemed rather supernatural to me, a guidepost from above.

In time, though, my anxieties resurfaced again, but a second confirmation came during a Bible Study Fellowship lecture by Bill Wierenga. As I sat in a pew on this particular Monday night, listening to his message, I could barely believe my ears. He was speaking about God's guiding providence in our lives by recounting the story of his own engagement, which sounded so similar to ours, even down to our personalities. He shared how he had been full of anxiety and doubt and how God had provided guideposts that calmed his nerves and confirmed his decision, resulting in many happy years of marriage. Little did he know that his story was being used that very night in the same way for me.

My last confirmation (I'm embarrassed to admit I needed yet another) was the most unusual, and, thankfully, it steadied my heart for good.

It was a Saturday night, and I was up most of the night tossing and turning, praying that God would calm my nerves and help me to trust him. At 6:00 a.m., my phone rang. It was a friend,

Pattie, whom I hadn't stayed connected with much. She had been in our young-adult singles group at Bella Vista Church in Rockford, Michigan, but had since married and moved to Ohio. To get a call from her was somewhat unusual, but to get a call from her so early on a Sunday morning was—well, you get the idea.

"Mitch, this is Pattie Dooley. I'm sorry to call you so early, but the Lord put you on my heart and gave me this message for you: You're doing the right thing in marrying Chris!"

> *There have been plenty of times in my life when he chose to be silent even though I wanted him to direct me in some way. And yet, although he's not obligated, there are times when he intervenes.*

Pattie was not part of our circle and, without the invention of social media, had no way to know that I was struggling. For her to call when I was at my worst was the best thing that could have happened to me. There was absolutely no question God was in this and he was guiding us toward marriage. This past year, Chris and I celebrated thirty-two years of marriage, and each year I get a fun note from Pattie: "I knew it was meant to be!"

God doesn't always show himself to us. There have been plenty of times in my life when he chose to be silent even though I wanted him to direct me in some way. And yet, although he's not obligated, there are times when he intervenes, and those times stand as a testament to his love and care for his children.

> "Because of the tender mercy of our God . . .
> the rising sun will come to us from heaven
> to shine on those living in darkness and
> in the shadow of death, to guide our feet
> into the path of peace." (Luke 1:78–79)

16

Always Growing, Never Arriving

I discovered early in the faith journey that my faith could never stand the test of time if I sought to go it alone. I knew the commitment I made to follow Jesus on that mid-July night in 1979 was lifelong. So as a young eighteen-year-old, I set out to build a life that would give me the best chance to stay true to that commitment, a life that would be able to weather the storms that I would have to pass through. I knew I would fail and fall and have to get back up again and again. Would I be able to forgive myself? Would I be strong enough to avoid abandoning the faith and returning to a lifestyle of sin and selfishness? There would be so many traps to navigate—pleasure, lust, materialism, pride—alongside challenges of pain, hurt, anger, resentment. Somehow I knew that *where* I positioned myself and *who* I positioned myself with would make all the difference. Scripture guided me to "spur one another on toward love and good deeds, not giving up meeting together . . . but encouraging one another—and all the more as you see the Day approaching" (Hebrews 10:24–25).

In the early years of my faith journey, I endured internal suffering, a byproduct of my repentance, the whiplash of a life redirected. I cut myself off from partying, drinking, and playing, in exchange for companionship, study, and prayer. I severed ties with individuals that had no interest in pursuing holiness over indulgence. This was painful for me, and there were times of true regret. Yes, regret. I missed my old life terribly. I wanted to go back, not unlike a drug addict who has gone through rehab and has to endure periods of desperate desire to return to the old hurtful habits. I suffered through these times because I knew the fun of sin never lasted and always left me bitter, not better (Proverbs 26:11). Not that I never sinned again, of course I did. I would veer off from time to time and still do, but I always found my way back, whether on my own or with the help of a close friend who cared too much to allow me to wander from my faith. In my late teens, I could be found on the weekends in a study with a group of guys reading *The Pursuit of Holiness* by Jerry Bridges. We each wanted a fresh start. We not only wanted to be different but also desired to find spouses that were grounded in the same faith we had found, spouses who could navigate the path with us.

I recently heard someone say, "Some go to church because that is what good people do, while others go because they know they are not good." I always want to be found in that latter group. It took me awhile to sort this out. My behavior had changed because I had the power of God within me and I was growing in my relationship with him. But sin was always, and still is, close by . . . just a thought away, a slip of the tongue, a cruel word. And even if I manage to make it through a day without sinning, I'm still a sinner, for that is my nature. I also, however, possess a new nature that has become my true self. I have been born again through God's Spirit who has taken up residence within me. I have the power to cast off the old and live into the new, knowing full well the old will rear its head again. Yet I can rest in the knowledge this is no longer me, rather it is the old self that will not survive and, in fact, is dying a slow death. I will never find my sinless footing until I move from this life to the next. I take heart in my sin awareness; that is to say, awareness of my depravity is the very thing that causes me to cling to the cross. As soon as I feel I am good in myself or good enough, I am the most lost. (Romans 7:24, 25).

Early on in my faith, I was attending Bella Vista Church. On one particular Sunday, a friend of mine, Ken, approached me and showed me some notes from his notebook. He was very enthusiastic about a class he had discovered called Bible Study Fellowship (BSF). I glanced down at his notebook. The detailed notes resembled a college course more than a light Bible study. I wasn't interested. Ken was very diligent and persistent and either didn't pick up on my signals or chose to ignore them. A year later, he finally wore me down, and I agreed to join him for an intro class. I figured I could then say, "Hey, I tried it. It's not for me," and be done with it. To my surprise, I really enjoyed the class and decided to go back the next week and the next and the next. I realized both how little I really knew the content of the Bible and how much the Bible had to say about how I lived my day-to-day life. The power was in the application.

As I write this, I can honestly say the decision I made to commit myself to the serious study of Scripture has changed my life more than any other decision I have made. For to walk in the way, one needs to be found in the way, and that only happens through the Word. In John 1:1, we find that Jesus was called the Word. I discovered that being acquainted with the Bible was the path to knowing God. And knowing God leads to discovering his purpose for my life. Without this knowledge, I would wander aimlessly through life and easily be pulled anywhere, especially with flawed or skewed doctrines. With strong biblical knowledge, I was directed by his hand, not tossed around like a rag doll and influenced by false teachings (Ephesians 4:14).

I wanted to be intentional with my life, much like the folktale of the man named Christian in the book *Pilgrim's Progress.* Christian has a dream, and in the dream, he finds himself on a perilous journey that ends at heaven's gate. John Bunyan penned this allegory in 1678 and it became an immediate top seller—number one behind the Bible for decades actually. A vivid depiction of the Christian journey, this 340-year-old book struck a chord with me as he illustrated the difference between true and false faith and all the accompanying risks of the journey. A journey that, in reality, all followers of Christ are on. Yet so often we can be lulled to sleep through the intoxication of busy lives or lives that become busy as a way to avoid spiritual reflection. As I look over my life, I can identify with the detours Christian took and how he found his way back to the road again and again. In large part, his familiarity with the road map—the Bible—guided him, protecting him from wandering too far.

The thing I love the most from the stories of the New Testament is the grace-filled redemption of the sinful, sick, and discarded people. "I have not come to call the righteous, but sinners to repentance," says Jesus (Luke 5:32). I don't know of any words more hopeful than those. Those words make me so thankful for my acute awareness of my sinful state. I know deeply that I will never graduate into wholeness, holiness, or perfection in this life. Sure, I have come a long way (because of Jesus), yet I am still imperfect. I am resting in my brokenness, knowing that Jesus stands in the gap between who I am and the righteousness God requires. It's as if I can relax a bit, knowing my best efforts are virtually worthless. Any good within me is him and all good is from him. The fact I get to participate in the process is mind-bending. There is no place for pride, never, ever.

I recall reading a story of a man of faith, a man that had been in the ministry for most of his life. A man who sought hard after God and was a man of God. He was old and dying. As he lay in his hospital bed, terrible thoughts and images rushed through his mind—sinful, lustful, disgusting thoughts, thoughts that were decades removed from who he believed he had become. He immediately began praying, "Lord, deliver me from these thoughts!" And just as he was praying, the Lord spoke to his heart, "Take a good look at yourself. This is who you are apart from me."

I have never forgotten that story. It is so comforting to me because as much as I want to be or to project I have it together, as much as I hope to mature into a man of God, I am reminded I am a sinner who happens to have found Christ. I didn't fully understand it at the time of my conversion, but my life was forever revolutionized by his grace. As the shame of my agnostic days fell away, it was replaced with a deep love

It's paradoxical: the greater the amount of sin that needs forgiveness, the greater the portion of grace and love that is poured out.

for Christ. It's paradoxical: the greater the amount of sin that needs forgiveness, the greater the portion of grace and love that is poured out. My life was brimming with transgressions, but rather than shame or guilt, I was flooded with joy. As if it were a by-product of a *grace + sin* equation. I loved Christ for what he accomplished on the cross not only on my own behalf but also on behalf of others. I felt then, and even more today, a burden for those who don't know him to experience the same forgiveness, joy, and grace that I have. Maturing in my faith was no more or less than reading and applying the Word of God and allowing the truth to radically change my view of myself, my neighbors, and my purpose here on this earth.

"Therefore, I tell you, her many sins have been forgiven—as her great love has shown. But whoever has been forgiven little loves little." (Luke 7:47)

BIBLICAL
TRUTHS

17

Light in the Shadows

In the shadows of the night, timid about being seen yet brave to seek out truth, a highly accomplished teacher searches out the controversial Jesus. What motivated Nicodemus to seek out Jesus in solitude during the evening hours? Was he in search of a new truth? Was he captivated by the miracles? Did he really believe this man, Jesus, had come from God? Whatever it was, he sought his answers in the security of the shadows.

Jesus begins their time together with an answer to a question Nicodemus had not yet asked, the truth he knew Nicodemus was seeking: "Very truly I tell you, no one can see the kingdom of God unless they are born again" (John 3:3).

Nicodemus did not hide his confusion as he would have in the light of day. "How can someone be born when they are old? . . . Surely they cannot enter a second time into their mother's womb to be born!" (v. 4).

Jesus reveals the necessity of a spiritual rebirth, comparing those born of the Spirit with the wind—no longer directed by the predictable nature of the flesh but by the unpredictable Spirit-nature of God.

Hearing this, Nicodemus blurts out, "How can this be?" (v. 9). These words are the last record of him speaking that night.

The rest of the evening and into the days, weeks, and months ahead, Nicodemus must have been churning over Jesus's challenge. Listen to how Jesus responds to Nicodemus: "You are Israel's teacher . . . and do you not understand these things?" (v. 10).

Truth missed by those who were in the business of dispensing truth—Nicodemus was not the only Jewish teacher to be schooled by Jesus. Elsewhere in John's Gospel, Jesus says to a group of Jewish leaders, "You study the Scriptures diligently because you think that in them you have eternal life. These are the very Scriptures that testify about me, yet you refuse to come to me to have life" (John 5:39–40). How terrifying that these teachers of the law hadn't recognized Jesus in the text and now refused him in the flesh and opposed him in the courts. What a vast difference there is between coming to Jesus and merely knowing how to study religion!

Jesus extends an invitation for Nicodemus to recalibrate his faith. His message is simple: Unless you believe in me, you will have missed everything. All you have worked for, all you have studied, all you have denied yourself will come to nothing. It is a simple belief, yet profoundly easy to trip over. "But we preach Christ crucified: a stumbling block to Jews and foolishness to Gentiles" (1 Cor. 1:23).

Ultimately, Nicodemus fully comes to Jesus and experiences being born again, a spiritual awakening. We find him bringing expensive oils to prepare the body of Jesus for the tomb. As surely as he found Jesus that evening in the shadows, he found him again in the light of his own spiritual rebirth. He was born again to prepare his Savior's lifeless body for his resurrection (John 19:39–42). This was the beautiful result of finding truth that had previously evaded him. This is what happens when we come to Jesus amidst our uncertainty.

Many will go through the motions of religious activity but miss the simple truth. It all starts with coming to Jesus, just as we are, and receiving what we cannot do for ourselves. Eternal life is awakened by a rebirth of our spirit through the blood sacrifice of God's Son. No matter your position or authority, when you miss that, you miss everything.

Many of the religious were spiritually bankrupt, even as the treasure, the very Son of God, was right in their midst. Jesus was the elephant in the room. Jesus is the one throughout the text, the one staring them in the face, yet the one they refused to personally face. Much of their blindness resulted from their pursuit of control, wealth, and position. They saw their first birth as preeminent and a second, spiritual birth as unnecessary.

The religious, far from Jesus, are akin to men living above an oil field who are given a deed with an instruction manual detailing how to strike oil. They study the manual seriously but miss the section on how to extract the oil, and thus miss experiencing the riches. They end up wasting all their time studying about the oil and how the oil is the source of limitless wealth; however, they confuse accessibility with possession. The oil is available, but unless it is extracted and secured, it is worthless. Despite their proximity to abundance, they live poor and impoverished lives.

They confuse accessibility with possession.

Many of the religious of Jesus's day based their position on knowledge yet never dug deep for rebirth through Jesus. They felt no need to search out Jesus, who offered an inconvenient truth of a spiritual rebirth. Embracing the truth of Jesus meant exchanging possessions, positions, and piety for freedom, grace, and humility.

My rebirth experience came in mid-July, the summer of

1979. At age eighteen, I realized how futile my life had become. I was awakened to a spiritual realm beyond the life I knew. Bowing down by my bed and praying a simple prayer, all became new for me. The Word became living and active. My love for God became deep and meaningful. Everything changed—not just a new perspective but a whole new dimension. I was born again.

Rebirth is a finding of our true selves. We find our identity in the spiritual realm through Christ, not later but here and now in this life that will usher us into the next. Later is too late. Jesus came as our sacrifice and Lord with a generous invitation to experience the riches of rest.

> "Come to me, all you who are weary and
> burdened, and I will give you rest." (Matt. 11:28)

18

Look Both Ways

The pounding was getting old, day after day, week after week. Months turned into years. Old man Noah and his family were written off by their surrounding neighbors as delusional killjoys.

When he wasn't sawing, planking, and pounding, Noah was preaching. He was a preacher of righteousness in a very unrighteous place. His message to his neighbors was always the same: "Repent! God's wrath has reached its limit! A flood is coming that will destroy the world!" This was his calling, to build an ark, preach truth, and warn the people. The effect? Laughter followed by ridicule and mockery. They'd walk away, right back to their sinful lifestyles. Their hearts were hard, their ways were wicked, and their greed-filled appetites drove them further and further away from salvation. This was the scene prior to the greatest natural disaster the world had ever experienced. A warning not heeded.

Christ preached a similar warning to crowds centuries later. He warned of a day ahead like the days of Noah. This warning was for the listening crowds as well as for generations stretching centuries into the future. In Luke 17:26 Jesus says, "Just as it was in the days of Noah, so also will it be in the days of the Son of Man." And in verse thirty he continues, "It will be just like this on the day the Son of Man is revealed." It was a strange warning at the time Jesus issued it, stranger yet for our generation, being so much more removed from the days of Noah.

I have found myself laughing inside at the cardboard warning signs held up by the religious fanatics at various public events, or the annoying bullhorn preachers warning the passersby of their impending destiny of hell and brimstone. These methods seem so extreme. I know Jesus often warned his listeners of judgment and hell, yet I imagine his tone to be soft and full of empathy as he spoke.

A warning is a warning, regardless of the approach or the delivery. If judgment is coming, does tone and delivery really matter? If you came to work and got word your company was going to close its doors, it wouldn't much matter whether it was announced in a memo, over a loudspeaker, or in the soft voice of an HR director. The message would be all that mattered. And I guarantee the talk around the water cooler would not be about who delivered the message in the best way. It would be the message, not the method, that would concern you.

When we hear these warnings today, could it be the reason we talk about the messenger or the method is that we don't believe the actual message? If we truly believed the warning, we would place our focus entirely on the content of the message.

Perhaps the fact so few are talking about the return of Jesus is a sure sign that it's imminent? After all, he said he would come when we least expect it, like a thief in the night. It's so hard to imagine his return in the normal rhythms of life. We know few will expect it or be prepared for it, making it all the more difficult to stand in the minority, looking up with anticipation.

I believe another factor in our lax attitude toward his return as a judge is our preferred focus on his love and grace attributes. Do we ignore his justice and wrath attributes to our own peril? Something that was preached loud and strong in past generations, to the point of being overly emphasized, is now under-emphasized today. Pendulums swing from side to side, but true balance is found in the Bible, where judgment and grace abound in equal measure throughout the Old and New Testaments alike.

It is so tempting to live only under the umbrella of grace. Clearly, Jesus ushered this in and demonstrated grace in his love for the unlovable, his forgiveness to those steeped in sin. But he also made these statements: Go and sin no more. Stop sinning or something worse may happen to you. If your hand causes you to sin, cut it off. He extended grace, yes, but often stern warnings would follow these grace moments. His most cutting words were always directed at the hypocrites, at the actors of the faith. These leaders could walk out on the stage of life and bring down the house with pious religiosity, all the while harboring greed and wickedness just under their surface. Jesus held nothing back when addressing them: "Woe to you, teachers of the law and Pharisees, you hypocrites! You are like whitewashed tombs, which look beautiful on the outside but on the inside are full of the bones of the dead and everything unclean" (Matt. 23:27).

Either we are living a lie and fooling everyone but God, or we are living authentically and not attempting to hide our sin.

Either we are living a lie and fooling everyone but God, or we are living authentically and not attempting to hide our sin. Either way, we could use a healthy fear of God mixed with an understanding of his grace.

A mother never stops warning her youngster to look both ways when crossing the street. Likewise, we need to look both ways as we step through life, not just looking down the grace lane of the road but turning to see the wrath and judgment side as well, for ourselves and for others in our lives. The first time I was in London, I was surprised by the warning signs painted on the road at each intersection. They read, LOOK THIS WAY, with an arrow pointing toward the right. Apparently, they had a significant problem with Western tourists stepping into traffic because they weren't accustomed to cars driving on the left side of the road. It was unnatural to look right, so these warning signs saved lives. We, too, need warning signs that point us away from spiritual dangers running counter to our nature.

It is one thing to want God's nature to be or not to be a certain way; it's a very different thing to not accept and submit to him just as he is. This is how we love God, all sides of him, even the parts we have yet to fully understand. We can only know in part as long as we are on this side of heaven. "'For my thoughts are not your thoughts, neither are your ways my ways,' declares the Lord. 'As the heavens are higher than the earth, so are my ways higher than your ways and my thoughts than your thoughts'" (Isa. 55:8–9).

Based on this verse, if God's ways make sense to us and align with our ways, then we have a distorted view of God—distorted, because his ways do not align with ours. Loving God is loving a divine deity who is beyond comprehension and vastly different from us.

Loving God is similar to our earthly relationships: we know there will be tension and misunderstanding, but standing firm and working through it is the very path of love. Loving God is a path that requires looking both ways—grace and judgment.

19

Repent

I stood there looking out over an auditorium full of men dressed alike in uniform, prison-issued clothes. I had the privilege of speaking that night and I wanted to bring a message of hope and healing.

As I prayed about it and began working on my message during the weeks leading up to it, the word *repent* kept coming to my mind. At first, I rejected the word because of the implications it might hold. I mean, really? Tell a group of men, forty percent of whom are in this prison for murder, that they need to repent? How is that going to be a message of hope? The men coming to this service, I reasoned, were coming because they had established a relationship with Jesus. Hadn't they taken care of repenting a long time ago? These were my arguments to God for not wanting to preach on repentance.

Yet the word kept surfacing, so I went with it and developed my talk around it. Only as I began to get deeper into my message did I understand why this word was appropriate—and yes, hope filled—for these men. Below are some excerpts from my message to them.

Jesus had much to say and teach everywhere he went. However, there was one word that stood out among all others, and it was the word *repent*. It's an interesting word; some would even consider it a command. It's interesting because it was the word boldly broadcasted by the one who came before Jesus. The centerpiece word of John's message that prepared the way for the Messiah was just this: repent! John the Baptist was not an ordinary man—far from it. In fact, Jesus said of all men born of a woman, John was the greatest.

John could be found in the wilderness, always with this bold pronouncement: "Repent, for the kingdom of heaven has come near!" (Matt. 3:2). And when Jesus began preaching, even before he picked his disciples, he made the same statement, word for word: "Repent, for the kingdom of heaven has come near!" (Matt. 4:17).

Repentance is paramount to our faith, the first and essential step in establishing or re-establishing our relationship with God. Miss this step and we miss God and all he has for us. True repentance is necessary for everyone, not just for bona fide sinners. Often, we compare ourselves to others and evaluate ourselves by their measure, as if somehow we are good enough so long as we are significantly better than the worst among us or perhaps slightly better than the average sinner. Unfortunately, we are all the worst. All have fallen short. If our journey to God required a hundred-foot leap across a massive canyon, it wouldn't matter much if you could jump five feet farther than the person next to you, would it? Given the distance between our sinful state and God's perfect, holy state, we are all hopeless to bridge the gap in our own strength or effort. God has to come to us, which he did in Jesus. Jesus has to be received, which he is through repentance.

I came across a wonderful example of how repentance is necessary for all of us. Listen to Jesus's words: "Those eighteen who died when the tower in Siloam fell on them—do you think they were more guilty than all the others living in Jerusalem? I tell you, no! But unless you repent, you too will all perish" (Luke 13:4–5).

You know what Jesus would say if he were speaking tonight? The same thing: Do you think the men in MCF are worse sinners than those throughout Muskegon? I tell you, no! But unless you repent, you all will perish!

You see, all people need to repent. If a person looks good to society, that does not make him or her good. In fact, those who are covering hidden sin are in the worst shape, because they have deceived themselves and those around them. Often, they are the ones who won't come to Jesus, and Jesus can't get to them or get their attention. These individuals were lost in Jesus's day, and they are lost today. They simply don't recognize their need to repent, despite Jesus's clear message: unless you repent, you will all perish. *All* leaves no one out.

How is it that so many have failed—and still fail—to see this? What was true then is true today: those who have clearly sinned, more clearly understand their need for repentance.

Take Saul, for example. Prior to his conversion, Saul was, at best, a misguided religious leader who was zealous for his cause; at worst, he was a man who committed premeditated murder and approved the stoning of Stephen, a follower of Jesus (Acts 8:1). How can it be, then, that Jesus later chose him to be his instrument to proclaim Christ to the Gentile world? After Saul's face-to-face encounter with Jesus on the road to Damascus and his name change to Paul, he suffered greatly for the cause of Christ. He wrote letters, now contained in the canon of Scripture, from a prison cell (yes, a prison cell). He was in prison for the cause of Christ, but he knew he deserved to be there for his murderous transgressions against Christians. He felt the shame of his transgression, weeping over those he had hurt and killed. Though he was, by his own admission, the chief among sinners (1 Tim. 1:15–16), God used him, a man guilty of grievous sin, to greatly advance his kingdom.

Saul came face-to-face with Jesus on the Damascus road, and his response was to repent. We all have our Damascus road story. We have all repented or perhaps still need to repent. Jesus is calling all of humankind into repentance. It's not about what you have done or where you have come from; it's about all of us being sinners who are born with the sin nature and are in need of a Savior. Those who know they need forgiveness are the ones who will come to Jesus—the friend of sinners (Luke 7:34). Those who don't see themselves as sinners will opt out of needing or receiving Jesus, making them truly lost.

> *Those who don't see themselves as sinners will opt out of needing or receiving Jesus, making them truly lost.*

Tonight, or sometime before tonight, you may have moved through the process of repenting and receiving Jesus. Or perhaps you are still on the Damascus road. I pray that Jesus will meet you as he did me and will interrupt your life with the most life-giving interruption, hearing and responding to the simple call: "Repent, for the kingdom of heaven has come near!" Yes, he is here with us tonight, always awaiting our response, always knocking on our door, always ready to abide with us and carry us home across the gap that only he can bridge.

I hope you see that hope is in him. Hope comes to the best and worst of us. And just as all are called to repent, all who do repent are made perfect in him. There is no greater hope, no greater reward. He is our reward as we, in our renewed state, receive him—the perfecter of our faith (Heb. 12:2), the one we will be like on the day he returns.

Dear friends, now we are children of God, and what we will be has not yet been made known. But we know that when Christ appears, we shall be like him, for we shall see him as he is. All who have this hope in him purify themselves [repent], just as he is pure. (1 John 3:2–3)

20

Where's the Meaning?

"You are going to die. I am going to die. We're all going to die, and it doesn't matter if it's tomorrow or eighty years from now." This was Siggy's line in the 1991 movie *What about Bob?* The young boy Siggy is obsessing over death and expresses his phobia to Bob. Though he is young, Siggy has become aware of the reality of death, obsessed by its universality, and begins to question continuing to live.

I can identify with Siggy. As a boy of seven, I had a similar phobia, although it was not so much a fear of death as a fear of not knowing my purpose. I was hit with an overwhelming anxiety over the question, "Why am I here?" I would meditate on that question and come up empty, which would fill me with fear. I felt lost and separated from everyone during those anxiety attacks. I can still feel the pangs of fear when I think back on those times and that question. This kind of anxiety is strikingly similar to the laments in the book of Ecclesiastes.

"Meaningless! Meaningless!" says the Teacher. "Utterly meaningless! Everything is meaningless." What do people gain from all their labors at which they toil under the sun? Generations come and generations go, but the earth remains forever. (Eccl. 1:2–4)

If King Solomon, the wisest man in the Old Testament, obsessed over the meaning—or rather, the meaninglessness—of life, those of us who have similar anxiety are in good company. Few of us go through life without anxiety over our purpose for being. In our day and age, it is so easy to become exasperated when we see the senselessness of all that is happening around us. We live in an instant-information age that feeds us a steady diet of illogical tragedy, whether catastrophic natural disasters hitting unsuspecting people, the next mass shooting, global warming, or human trafficking, the list goes on.

Desensitization has become the default coping mechanism for most of us. How else can we cope with so much overwhelming bad news coming at us from every angle? Perhaps Siggy and Solomon's conclusion that life is void of meaning is the only conclusion when catastrophes abound and death is a surety for us all.

Is suffering always a direct result of sin? In John 9:1–2 the disciples inquire of Jesus regarding a blind man, "Rabbi, who sinned, this man or his parents, that he was born blind?" Jesus was quick to point out, "Neither this man nor his parents sinned, but this happened so that the works of God might be displayed in him" (John 9:3). Or as referenced earlier, Jesus spoke about a disaster that took place at the tower in Siloam that claimed eighteen lives (Luke 13:4–5). He makes it clear that disasters can happen apart from cause and effect, pointing out that those who died were not more guilty than others who lived in Jerusalem. He is emphatic: "I tell you, no!" However, Jesus directs us to the first and vital step to finding our purpose: repentance. It was the message of John the Baptist and is the core theme of Jesus's preaching. It is the centerpiece word when the backdrop is disaster. It is the lifeline Jesus tosses out: do this to avoid perishing; do this and you will live. It is a restorative message: turn away from the way of destruction and you will flourish. In these few words, Jesus directs his audience, including us, to the one thing we must do to avoid disaster and a meaningless life—repent!

Life apart from relationship with God is meaningless beyond measure. Life in relationship with God is meaningful beyond measure. For many, this one act—repentance—stands in the way of entering into relationship with him. Webster defines *repent* as a turning from sin, dedicating oneself to the amendment of one's life. This vital step turns us away from sin and directs us toward God. Repentance opens up a future, rich in meaning, void of fear, and full of hope. Luke 12:32 guides us: "Do not be afraid, little flock, for your Father has been pleased to give you the kingdom."

> *Life apart from relationship with God is meaningless beyond measure. Life in relationship with God is meaningful beyond measure.*

21

Grace + Nothing

Imagine the scene in Genesis 11:1–9, sometime around 2240 BC, roughly a hundred years after the flood. At first glance, it appears to be vastly different from the present, but with a closer look, something immensely familiar is happening. God lives high above humans but has made known his will for humans to spread out and populate the earth (Gen 9:1). Humankind is not at all interested in obedience to God; instead, humans desire to do something great apart from God. They aspire to something they can point to and marvel at, but most of all to something about which they can say, "Look at what we have achieved on our own!" This fierce reliance on self has resounding spiritual implications, for not only are their efforts completed apart from God, but also they are, it turns out, in direct opposition to God's purposes.

The vision for this human-led accomplishment would only be possible by sticking together and not spreading out as God intended. The crowning achievement of their work in the great city would be a tower, one that would seemingly reach into the heavens where God resides, and where humans could reach that godlike place of being able to look out and down over all they had achieved. So they set out to build something extraordinary, not because of a desire to be with God but in order to prove their own greatness.

This is how the famed Tower of Babel story plays out, right up to the point where our merciful God stymies their plans by changing their languages, thus forcing them to abandon the project altogether. I find it interesting that humanity was given full freedom to create the plans and get deep into the project before the Divine intervenes. Was this God's grace to allow humans time to reconsider and perhaps change their minds? Was it to allow humanity to feel a greater sense of loss, leading to repentance and thus recalibration of their relationship with God? Whatever it was, we know that it was ultimately an act of mercy—just over a hundred years earlier the entire world was wiped out in the flood. This project would put all focus and praise on human accomplishment in opposition to God, a mix that is a time-tested recipe for wickedness and greed.

Isn't this always the struggle or tendency of being human: wanting so desperately to be the center of attention, the reason for one's own elevation, that to bring God into the project becomes not only inconvenient but unnecessary and, truth be told, even undesirable? While humans don't often admit this struggle, we do tend to use token prayers, requesting God to bless this work or that work as artificial evidence that God is in the works of our hands.

So easily blinded by ego are we that we unwittingly compete with God for the credit, even when it comes to our own salvation. "Of course I'm saved. Look at the good thing I am building for God!"—as if God is the one who is fortunate to have us doing his work. But in so doing, humanity is discrediting Jesus's completed work, are we not? As Jesus himself says in Matthew's

Gospel, "Many will say to me on that day, 'Lord, Lord, did we not prophesy in your name and in your name drive out demons and in your name perform many miracles?' Then I will tell them plainly, 'I never knew you. Away from me, you evildoers!'" (Matt. 7:22–23). So much for earning our own way!

Fast-forward from the scene in Genesis 11 to the time of Christ's crucifixion. Imagine a mighty structure built by Christ, its giant columns made of hardened steel, reaching all the way to God, to his heavenly dwelling place. This structure represents the work done by Christ on the cross, work that transports humans to his Father in heaven.

Now imagine a different tower, constructed by humans, using inadequate materials and tools, relying on human effort in an attempt to reach God. This tower, unlike Christ's perfect tower, serves only one purpose: to show humans our inadequacy to achieve true greatness or to reach God by our own means. The human-made tower represents the Old Testament law, which served to show humanity's sinful state, not remove it, and to demonstrate our human inability to reach God on our own. Clearly, we are not up to the task. The building standards are just too high, too lofty.

Someone had the idea to rewrite the building standards. By making the standards easily attainable and lowering the tower height, maybe they could succeed. Perhaps being careful not to add anything to the code that was not achievable would allow them to reach their goal. This seemed right to humans, an exceptional idea that many bought into despite having to diminish their God to a "god" in the process (few seemed to notice). Away they went with their little tower project! The men working on the project became proud and arrogant, often looking down in judgment on those who weren't part of it, saying, "I'm so glad we're not like them with their little sticks, trying to measure up to our tower."

Imagine Jesus, the ultimate building inspector, surveying the project built by the hands of such proud humans. Did they even recognize Jesus, whose standards had been written out of the code so long ago? The original, unachievable standard had long been forgotten. Jesus was saddened by the wholly inadequate structure, saddened that his tower stood ready but was largely ignored. He reminded them of the original code and the only builder able to build the structure they desired; only faith in him would grant them access to the Father. They felt threatened by this stumbling block (1 Cor. 1:23) and asked him to leave.

Still, those who put their faith in him were lifted up and set on the solid platform. Many were compelled to do something to earn this position, but they were assured that the work had already been done. Some were like freed slaves who occasionally still felt like slaves, needing time to live into their freedom.

Some, out of curiosity, had wandered over to the base of Christ's structure but still refused to put their faith in him. Rather, in their strength, they tried to scale it but slipped down, tried to nail into it but the nails broke down.

> To be lifted up requires the dropping of all our tools and methods to reach God.

Countless souls simply refuse to put their faith in Jesus, his work, and his sacrifice on their behalf. Insisting they add to the process, they miss salvation altogether. To be lifted up requires the dropping of all our tools and methods to reach God. As humans, we must destroy our idols and put our faith, an unashamed faith, in Christ's finished work of redemption.

Babel happened in ancient times, yet some four thousand years later, the struggle remains. Maybe the scene at Babel isn't so different than the scene today in our modern twenty-first century. Perhaps it's just our tools, technology, and culture that have changed. As much as we are inclined to oppose it, we still find our salvation and freedom through grace alone—grace plus nothing!

Yet the struggle with ego, so fundamental to our human condition, continues to be the same threat to our position in Christ today that it was at Babel. It requires humility to both see and receive our need for a Savior, a need that is met in Christ alone.

22

Hard to Swallow

How does one accept Jesus when his words are so hard to receive?

He spoke of, and warned of, hell more than anyone throughout the Scriptures, more than every other mention combined, in fact. He openly condemned false teachers whom many held up as righteous. He was direct, some might even say rude, as he called out his disciples when they showed incomplete faith. He required absolute and complete loyalty. He stated truth without regard for the fallout. He made statements he knew would be misunderstood, and he said them anyway.

We wear wristbands that say WWJD?—What Would Jesus Do?—but in reality, we cannot or will not do what Jesus did in the way that Jesus did it. We are unlikely to say what Jesus said in the way he said it. So what is the point of asking? I understand the intent. It's a nice reminder to think about Jesus before we make decisions and to weigh each decision in light of what we believe Jesus would do. But if our lives are not in step with Jesus, does the reminder to consider what he would do make sense?

Are we prepared to do what he would do? Are we willing to do it? There are a myriad of things Jesus did that we, as his followers, were never intended to do, like forgive sin, heal at will, cast demons into pigs, call out hypocrisy by discerning an individual's internal motives, read people's minds, and the list goes on.

Regrettably, asking "What would Jesus do?" as if I might do it is akin to asking what I should have for dinner while I am standing in the middle of a desert. I can ask the question, but if I am not in a place to be able to enact or realize the answer, the question has diminished or even has no meaning at all.

We struggle with the complete Jesus. I do not think our struggle is as much about trying to be like Jesus as it is about fully accepting Jesus. Francis Chan, during the writing of his book *Erasing Hell*, realized he was embarrassed by some of the things Jesus said and he simply ignored those words. He said, "Like the nervous kid who tries to keep his friends from seeing his drunken father, I have tried to hide God at times."

If we were honest, we would admit we all struggle with Jesus's rough edges and his damning language. Additionally, we struggle with his directives for our lives. So we hide behind the culture card. Surely, his words were meant for the time and space he lived in, not for today's modern culture? We listen to those who have platforms and assume, because of their education, intellect, or stage presence, they have the answers. And, of course, they do, but are those answers the complete picture?

We soak in the God-loves messages as if the wrath side of God does not exist. Meanwhile, Jesus speaks in clear, simple language and spends a great deal of his time warning people. My son Luke is playing Division II football. Luke is fully aware of the dangers of this sport and comes prepared each week for a battle. He always has aches and pains after games because of the physical nature of the sport. Now, if he were told he was signing up for flag or touch football, but it ended up being a contact sport, the first sustained hit would rock his world because he would not have seen it coming and would not have been prepared for it. This is often how I feel when I crack open the Bible. While I have been playing the noncontact sport of cultural Christianity all week, I'm hit with the words of Jesus and knocked right off my feet.

We want Jesus to somehow be different. We focus on his soft side, the image of him we can accept—even if it means an image we create for him. Often that image is informed and supported by our culture, which tends to shape him according to only one side of his character. We try to freeze him there and pretend the other side doesn't exist.

Imagine approaching marriage in this way. Wouldn't it be wonderful if you could freeze the aspects of your mate that you enjoy and ignore or avoid the rest? But love is not like that. Love means accepting all sides always. Although the analogy is weak and incomplete, it does drive home the point that our love for God is shaped by accepting the things that are hard to accept, knowing one day we will understand why they are there.

... dropping dollars into a plate in exchange for messages that will relieve guilt rather than convict with the full truth of Scripture ...

He lived a life of poverty, homelessness, and rejection, yet many today worship him from beautiful homes and sprawling megachurches—dropping dollars into a plate in exchange for messages that will relieve guilt rather than convict with the full truth of Scripture—a truth that demands lives of total sacrifice and complete surrender.

Perhaps we should stop asking the WWJD question as it relates to our life circumstances and simply look at what he did. He became a servant. He sacrificed himself. He prayed prayers of complete surrender and lived his life in obedience to the will of his Father. How dare we wear a bracelet with a message we have already chosen not to follow? We cannot do what Jesus did, but we can allow Jesus access to our lives. We can fully submit to him. We can do what he directs us to do, even if it means running counter to every grain of our culture. In fact, he tells us we can do even greater things than he did (John 14:12–14). What is Jesus desiring to do through you?

> "If anyone causes one of these little ones—those who believe in me—to stumble, it would be better for them if a large millstone were hung around their neck and they were thrown into the sea. If your hand causes you to stumble, cut it off. It is better for you to enter life maimed than with two hands to go into hell, where the fire never goes out. And if your foot causes you to stumble, cut it off. It is better for you to enter life crippled than to have two feet and be thrown into hell. And if your eye causes you to stumble, pluck it out. It is better for you to enter the kingdom of God with one eye than to have two eyes and be thrown into hell, where 'the worms that eat them do not die, and the fire is not quenched.'" (Mark 9:42–48)

23

Where's the Hell?

It seems the topic of hell is now taboo in our Western culture. If it weren't for profanity, the word might disappear altogether. It has all but been erased, even within most churches. The context of hell as an actual place seems to be voiced by the occasional street preacher or the crazy-eyed, billboard-clad, bullhorn-carrying Holy Roller. The latter sets up shop at large gatherings, and in a pious, self-righteous tone warns everyone of their eternal damnation in the burning lake of fire. Even if everyone fell to their knees and repented, he would likely just keep right on screaming condemnation. It's uncanny how he somehow knows that every single person within earshot is engaged in terrible sin, living far from God and headed straight to hell. How sad that his approach is so completely twisted and full of condemnation and hate. He gives heaven and hell a bad name and certainly does not represent the love of Christ whatsoever!

Every now and then, there's a mention of hell at the church we attend (ours is the exception not the rule, in my experience).

On the one hand, it makes sense that most folks, including pastors, don't want a steady diet of hellfire and brimstone. But on the other hand, why is a topic that was so central to Jesus's teaching so avoided in teaching and preaching today? Yes, it's uncomfortable (to say the least) but does that give us permission to avoid it as much as we do, hoping it will go away? Should we continue sweeping it back under the rug, only to have it occasionally creeping out into the light of day? I want to, I really do. But should we? Should I?

Growing contingents are pivoting away from viewing hell as a real place where people go who don't know Christ, and are moving toward seeing hell as a metaphorical place or as a description of hellacious conditions on this side of the grave. It's just too hard to believe that God would send people to a place like hell as it's described in the Scriptures. One popular author, teacher, and former pastor has moved from believing in hell to saying he cannot worship a God who would send people to hell. So he has written hell out of his talks, podcasts, and books. I have listened closely to his arguments and have read his books, trying desperately to keep an open mind. I do understand his rationale, and I sincerely want to believe the way he does.

The problem I have with this theology is, well, the Bible. Granted, I have not gone to seminary, but I'm also not biblically illiterate. Again, I would love to believe that hell, the eternal fire, is reserved only for the devil and his angels (Matt. 25:41) and that people would never be sent there, ever. But I just can't get to the place where I see this as truth. The arguments all seem to be centered on human rationale—namely, that it can't be true based on human reasoning and not based on what the Bible actually says.

I personally hate the idea of hell. However, most arguments against the existence of hell do a terrible job of making their case on the basis of sound biblical theology and the biblical text itself. Their intentions may be noble and good, but they do nothing to change my view. Francis Chan's book *Erasing Hell*, for example, is an excellent read but also troubling, not just for the reader but also for Chan as he wrestles with the reality of this place he would rather avoid in his messages. We have to be so careful not to distort who God is by reason of our human logic alone.

> Who has measured the Spirit of the Lord, or what man shows him his counsel? (Isa. 40:13 ESV)

> "For my thoughts are not your thoughts, neither are your ways my ways," declares the Lord. (Isa. 55:8)

I believe, against my own wishes and desires, in a literal hell, because of the overwhelming number of references to it and descriptions of it, along with Jesus's multiple warnings to avoid it. I think people would warm up to the idea of hell (no pun intended) if they took an honest look at the two sides of God. Sure, if I only look at the love, mercy, and grace side of God, I would never contemplate hell. The fact is, as beautiful and true as all those wonderful attributes are, they are not the complete picture. If I only look at the judgment and wrath side of God, I would never contemplate his love.

Focusing on only one side of God does not erase or diminish the existence of the other side of his character, but what it does do is limit our grasp of the full character of God.

Say I painted the right side of my car yellow and the left side blue. Then I drove down the street and later polled the people I passed on the right. They would all say my car was yellow and would be insistent on it. Meanwhile, the people on the left would be certain that my car, the same car, was blue. They would both be right! But they would also be wrong or only half right in their understanding. The truth is, my car is both yellow and blue. And the truth about God is that he is a God of love and wrath, mercy and judgment, forgiveness and unforgiveness. Focusing on only one side of God does not erase or diminish the existence of the other side of his character, but what it does do is limit our grasp of the full character of God.

Stepping back and looking at the whole of Scripture, we can't get very far before clearly seeing the two seemingly contradictory sides of God, a God who is unchanging—the same yesterday, today, and forever (Heb. 13:8). Early on in the book of Genesis, we see both sides of God. God blesses Adam and Eve. He provides a paradise garden with only one rule. When they break the rule, we see the judgment and punishment side of God. They are faced with the consequence of their sin. Not only could they not step foot back into the garden, but they were cursed by God. And we are still living with that curse today.

Later in Genesis, God spares Noah and saves him and his family but destroys the entire world population in a violent flood. Think about that: the entire population is wiped out by the hand of God, with only a handful spared because of the righteousness of Noah.

These are just two among the numerous accounts of God's wrath, judgment, and punishment. One might say, "Well, that is just the Old Testament. Jesus came and ushered in a gospel of grace and mercy, and now things are different." That is true, and it is wonderful beyond description. Yet God remains holy and just. Justice is righteousness.

In the New Testament, we see Jesus fashion a whip out of cords and use it to drive everyone from the temple courts in righteous anger (John 2:15). Ananias and Sapphira drop dead because they lie to the apostle about a gift amount for the church (Acts 5:1–11).

Decades ago, there was a much stronger focus from the pulpit on hell and judgment. I'm old enough to remember it. It was so depressing, and people seemed to walk away each Sunday under a pile of guilt and shame. Today there is a strong focus on God's grace, mercy, and love, and people walk away feeling perhaps better than they really should—not seeing the need for any change. The focus has shifted to God's love, no matter what, and boundaries and restrictions have become suggestions. Both of these extremes are dangerous.

As I struggle to come to grips with hell, I am reminded of a story I once heard of a man being hauled into a courtroom, guilty of the charges against him. Yet when it comes time for him to be sentenced, another man, who is innocent, comes forward and offers to take the first man's sentence: the death penalty. This is what Jesus did for us. He died a horrible death, took on the sins of the world, and faced complete separation from his Father. He took what we deserved. Yes, Jesus took the punishment for our sins, even before we committed them. And he now waits for us to decide. Will we defend ourselves in God's courtroom or take Jesus's substitutionary offer?

Instead of focusing on how unjust it is for God to send anyone to hell, consider how unfair it is to receive a complete pardon for sins you are guilty of committing. These are two ways of looking at the same coin. Not flipping the coin over, however, is a dangerous game, regardless of which side you choose to focus on. An inordinate focus on hell ignores God's grace and leaves us full of worry that we are under judgment. Too much focus on grace lets us off the hook for every decision and allows us to behave as if there are no consequences.

I am thankful Jesus calls us into a new birth. But that same Jesus makes it clear that to love him is to obey him and remain in him, just as he demonstrated his love for his Father through obedience and by being in his presence often in prayer. Obeying is how we love God, and it is ultimately the evidence of our faith.

24

Naked and Clothed in Preoccupation

They walked down the ramp single file, nothing in their hands nor on their persons. When they reached the end of the ramp, they were given a bundle of supplies, which included clothes, currency, and an instruction manual.

It was the first time any of these voyagers had been to this remote island. Surprisingly, no one questioned the destination or their reason for being there. They just gathered up their possessions (some had been given more than others) and went on their way to enjoy and develop their piece of the island. In addition to the written manual, a verbal notice was broadcast over speakers: "This is not your final home. You will be asked to return to the boat at any moment, so be ready at all times. You cannot take anything back with you from this island. Read your manual!"

Regrettably, few paid attention in their rush to get down to business and claim their territory before it was taken. The voice over the speakers faded as the people scurried off. The notice was repeated in the instruction manual, but many of the manuals were left scattered along the paths like discarded litter. All that seemed to matter was their place on the island, not why they were there in the first place.

In time, the island was a hub of activity. The busyness of their lives took precedence over any desire they might have had for reflective thinking. With so much to do and additional sections of the island to develop, there was no place for thoughtful introspection. Some built gigantic homes, while others could only afford the essentials, doing well just to have a roof over their head.

A small handful of island dwellers had embraced the verbal notice and guarded their manuals with their lives. This group was in no hurry to stake their claim on the island; rather they were driven by the purpose they discovered in the manual. These manual lovers formed a group and would meet often to review the manual, constantly discovering more of the purpose for their stint on the island. They read about how the island was under surveillance and how they would one day be accountable for the implementation of the clear instructions in the manual. They would be graded not for how much they had gained but for how much they had given to and cared for those who were hungry and hurting on the island. Some in this group would run around the island, warning others to read their manual. Most who heard would laugh and say things like, "Ha! That old, outdated thing? You need to get to work and stop wasting time."

So the hustle and bustle continued without pause—until it was a dweller's time to return to the boat, just as the manual had warned. A tap on the shoulder would signal to the (usually oblivious, preoccupied) dweller that it was time to go. He was then escorted back to the boat with nothing allowed in hand, often protesting the entire way, "This is a big mistake. Can't you see I was in the middle of something really important? You tapped the wrong person!" His protesting was disregarded by the soldiers on either side as they moved slowly and deliberately toward the boat. At the boat, the dweller was stripped to nothing and was walked up the long ramp he had previously descended. He passed an eager youth hustling down, whose eyes were running to and fro, taking in the views and anxiously anticipating his allotment at the ramp's end. This time, the dweller clearly heard the notice that had eluded his focus so many years earlier. "This is not your final home. You will be asked to return to the boat at any moment, so be ready at all times. You cannot take anything back with you from this island. Read your manual!"

Reality had sunk in while time had run out. What he wouldn't give for even a peek at the manual now and one more day to apply it.

His eagerness to make his own way on the island caused him to ignore the manual every day, right up to the end.

He knew it held the key and purpose for his time on the island. But it was too late now for introspection. He was ushered into a dim room. Sounds came from one end while the opposite end was lit up in bright white. A film started rolling. It was a film of this dweller's life and of his time spent on the island. He watched in horror, seeing how he lived for himself in every way, every day. The manual lay on the shelf in his room. His eagerness to make his own way on the island caused him to ignore the manual every day, right up to the end.

> Everyone comes naked from their mother's
> womb, and as everyone comes, so they depart.
> They take nothing from their toil that they
> can carry in their hands. (Eccl. 5:15)

> Just as people are destined to die once, and
> after that to face judgment . . . (Heb. 9:27)

25

Soul Battle

Satan ruled then and he rules now. But a time is coming when he will no longer rule at all, a time when he will be cast into the pit and tortured. He knows this, yet he continues in earnest to destroy humanity. The legion of demons fell before Jesus as the man they possessed shouted at the top of his voice, "What do you want with me, Jesus, Son of the Most High God? I beg you, don't torture me!" (Luke 8:28). They clearly knew, or had been told, their destiny, that they, along with every person who ever lived, would one day bow before Jesus, just like this man. For "at the name of Jesus every knee should bow, in heaven and on earth and under the earth, and every tongue acknowledge that Jesus Christ is Lord, to the glory of God the Father" (Phil. 2:10–11).

Paul says, "Our struggle is not against flesh and blood, but against the rulers, against the authorities, against the powers of this dark world and against the spiritual forces of evil in the heavenly realms" (Eph. 6:12). Though these are strange words to hear in this century, they are true nonetheless. Truth is always truth, regardless of our beliefs or the culture it finds itself in. Truth can be ignored in any number of ways, the most obvious of which today is by diverting our attention. A myriad of distractions push truth to the fringes of our minds. But truth, by its definition, cannot be diminished.

Hiding, distracting, ignoring, distorting—none of these change truth itself. Truth is that which it always was and always will be. Ultimately, it can't be debated away, twisted into, or hidden within partial replicas. No. Truth will stand untarnished in the end.

> *Hiding, distracting, ignoring, distorting— none of these change truth itself.*

Just like God, truth is the same yesterday, today, and forever. God is the ultimate truth, and his attributes always have been and always will be true. He is the great I Am. Before all else existed, I Am was there. God is not more or less alive today than he was before. He always was and always will be. He has taken the keys of our destruction away from the enemy of our souls, the hater of truth, and the father of lies.

God lives high above us, and our ways are not his ways. Yet we are created in his image. He chose to dwell not just among us but also within us. We are the holy temple of the Spirit of God. "Do you not know that your bodies are temples of the Holy Spirit, who is in you, whom you have received from God? You are not your own; you were bought at a price. Therefore honor God with your bodies" (1 Cor. 6:19–20).

God brings life, wholeness, and new beginnings to all who call upon him. It is too great to fathom! God is so tremendous that if a person stood in their fleshly state, even for a moment, in his presence, they would face immediate death. Moses sought to gaze upon him and could only glance at him from within the cleft of a rock as he passed by, exposing only a portion of his back side. Moses glowed for days after that fraction of an encounter. This is God, beyond human comprehension, while at the same time deeply desirous of us. This is God, yearning for a forever relationship with us. He seeks to save us from ourselves and from the enemy of our souls.

This enemy lives to kill and destroy. Like a roaring lion, he is always on the lookout for someone, anyone, to devour (1 Pet. 5:8). He will stop at nothing to destroy God's prized creation, us. Our enemy lives in the hidden spirit world, always planning, always observing, and continuously attempting to bring another to the end of their life. He benefits from people being unaware of him and his ways, either ignorant of God or with a view of God that is distorted (and usually dishonoring), agnostic, or a complete denial of God's existence. It really does not matter; so long as a genuine encounter with Jesus, the Savior of all, is avoided, the enemy has done his job.

Within the pages of Scripture, truth is revealed. C. S. Lewis in his book of essays attempts to describe people in the afterlife. He says that if we could see those who have rejected God, we would not be able to even look at them. The sight would be horrible beyond description, too painful to behold. Conversely, he says, if we could see those who have been found in Christ, we would fall on our knees and be tempted to worship them, for their heavenly form and countenance would be beautiful beyond our wildest imagination. This is truth. A truth that is both wonderful and awful. Every person you encounter this very day is going to be one or the other someday.

The heavenly realm is a realm of extremes. We have an enemy that is full of hatred, always against us, evil beyond our wildest imagination, and incomprehensibly dark. He battles day and night for the souls of humankind. Contrarily, God is holy, holy, holy. Our God is light, mercy, grace, and love. He offered his Son as a sacrifice so that all who receive him can be his children and be with him forever. His Holy Spirit battles against evil for human souls and has called us into the fight through prayer.

"And pray in the Spirit on all occasions with all kinds of prayers and requests. With this in mind, be alert and always keep on praying for all the Lord's people" (Eph. 6:18). We should pray with the knowledge of who we are, whose we are, and where we are. Positionally, we have joined Jesus. "And God raised us up with Christ and seated us with him in the heavenly realms in Christ Jesus" (Eph. 2:6). The truth is that people, all people, are what this battle is really about.

Funny how we can be in the midst of this battle and be so oblivious. If it weren't for scriptural reminders, would we find our way to an awareness? This heavenly battle isn't above us, it's around us—a battle for the souls of humankind fought primarily through prayer. Our prayers do make a difference. Each one is an affront to the enemy and fuel for our advocate. Each one reverberates across the heavens. Each one is a welcomed relief.

Lord, it is so easy for me to give my attention to everything but you and the battle you are waging for our souls. Yet you call me to awaken again to truth, a truth that beckons me to find myself in you. Help me to rest in that truth. May your Spirit be evident in me today. Help me to be engaged in the prayerful struggle against the powers of darkness in this world and the forces of evil that truly exist in the heavenly realm. Amen.

26

The Prerequisite

He that cannot forgive others breaks the bridge
over which he must pass himself,
for every man hath need to be forgiven.
−EDWARD HERBERT−

Forgiveness is not an easy thing to do. The fact that, biblically, I am required to perpetually forgive any and all who have wronged me is troubling. More troubling still is that our Father in heaven will not forgive us if we have not forgiven any and all who have wronged us. "But if you do not forgive others their sins, your Father will not forgive your sins" (Matt. 6:15). That is an amazingly difficult prerequisite to live up to. The dictionary defines *prerequisite* as a thing that is required as a prior condition for something else to happen or exist. So for me to experience forgiveness, forgiveness must flow through me perpetually. I'm pretty sure that is why it is central in the relatively short Lord's Prayer Jesus gave us.

Peter certainly struggled with Jesus's teaching on forgiveness.

Listen to his question in Matthew 18:21: "Lord, how many times shall I forgive my brother or sister who sins against me? Up to seven times?" It's funny he suggests a number to Jesus, almost like he's expecting to have to negotiate ("Okay, let's get this bidding started. How about up to seven?"). Jesus's answer must have shocked Peter. "I tell you, not seven times, but seventy-seven times" (v. 22). Sometimes this last phrase is translated as "seventy times seven," which makes me wonder whether Peter tried to do the math ("seventy times seven . . . let's see here, I think that would be 490 times—wait, *490 times*? Really?") or whether he got the point immediately. Either way, the number Jesus gave Peter must have seemed impossible.

Because forgiveness is such a big deal, Jesus continues his dialogue with Peter by telling a parable, which seems intended to sear into our minds the consequences of unforgiveness.

> "Therefore, the kingdom of heaven is like a king who wanted to settle accounts with his servants. As he began the settlement, a man who owed him ten thousand bags of gold was brought to him. Since he was not able to pay, the master ordered that he and his wife and his children and all that he had be sold to repay the debt.
>
> "At this the servant fell on his knees before him. 'Be patient with me,' he begged, 'and I will pay back everything.' The servant's master took pity on him, canceled the debt and let him go.
>
> "But when that servant went out, he found one of his fellow servants who owed him a hundred silver coins. He grabbed him and began to choke him. 'Pay back what you owe me!' he demanded.
>
> "His fellow servant fell to his knees and begged him, 'Be patient with me, and I will pay it back.'

"But he refused. Instead, he went off and had the man thrown into prison until he could pay the debt. When the other servants saw what had happened, they were outraged and went and told their master everything that had happened.

"Then the master called the servant in. 'You wicked servant,' he said, 'I canceled all that debt of yours because you begged me to. Shouldn't you have had mercy on your fellow servant just as I had on you?' In anger his master handed him over to the jailers to be tortured, until he should pay back all he owed." (Matt. 18:23–34)

This parable is downright frightening. It seems clear that forgiveness for anyone who has wronged us is not a suggestion; it is God's command, which should not be taken lightly. The principle of unforgiveness that is woven into the fabric of this story hits home for me; it's hard not to see myself in the narrative. When I consider my trespasses and how Jesus was the sacrifice required to wipe the slate clean, allowing me to live and not die in the next life, how can I possibly not forgive anyone who has trespassed against me, regardless of the offense or quantity of offenses? I am simply comparing mountains to molehills when I compare what God forgave to what I am required to forgive my fellow human for. How could I possibly stand before the Father and justify my right to not forgive a grievance when each one of my grievances

How could I possibly stand before the Father and justify my right to not forgive a grievance when each one of my grievances was taken care of at the cross?

was taken care of at the cross? That would certainly justify God's anger, would it not? All have been wronged, and all are called to forgive. Forgiveness is the mark of the saved, is it not?

I am reminded of a testimony I heard a while back that has

stuck with me. Jack was from New Zealand. He had wandered far from the faith, the faith of his mother. Jack had lived a wild life of sin, without a thought for others or for the consequences of his actions. While living in Europe, he was involved in a terrible car accident. He partially awakened on a gurney in the back of an ambulance. His spirit began to leave his body, and he knew he might not make it. It was in this partial spirit state the Lord appeared to Jack and let him know he had heard the faithful and numerous prayers of his mother back in New Zealand. These were prayers for Jack's salvation. Because of his mother's faithfulness, Jack was going to be granted a second chance. But there was one catch: there were two men that Jack had not forgiven over the course of his life. The Lord brought them to Jack's mind and said, "Are you willing to forgive these two?" As Jack shared this portion of his testimony, he became very serious. "As I lay there on that gurney, I struggled greatly to forgive these two men who had wronged me so, even though my very life depended on it." Eventually Jack was able to release the poison of unforgiveness, fully forgive these men, and then fully receive Christ's forgiveness. Jack made a full recovery and has since turned his life around.

This story is such a powerful message of forgiveness, redemption, and faithfulness on many levels. Forgiveness is so important, not just for later in the next life but for here and now. There are consequences to an unforgiving spirit that can and often do eat away at people. "Unforgiveness," says Joyce Meyer, "is like drinking poison and thinking the other person is going to die."

Jesus breaks it down in a single sentence of the Lord's Prayer. "Forgive us our sins, for we also forgive everyone who sins against us" (Luke 11:4). I see this as breathing in (receiving) the Lord's forgiveness and breathing out (giving) forgiveness to all. And I do mean all.

27

Escaping through Flames

He stood there feeling alone, entirely alone, and yet he was surrounded on all sides. Like a wheat field stretching endlessly in every direction, a massive assembly gathered around him. It was eerily quiet as he looked around in wonder at this spectacular sight.

He felt ill prepared. How could anyone fully prepare for this? His only awareness of what was about to take place came from a few passages of Scripture he'd heard in a Sunday school class decades ago. Those verses, he remembered, were extraordinary—and utterly odd. But they had never found their way into his day-to-day life. In fact, as his life moved forward, he had moved them into the attic of his mind, never to be pulled out, dusted off, or considered. Now though, as the moment described in those verses unfolded around him, he thought it a travesty he had not lived his life in preparation for this. How could this unavoidable event everyone will experience not have been front and center in his life on earth, and how was it not front and center in his church? While he waited, he reflected on the verses he had avoided.

> By the grace God has given me, I laid a foundation as a wise builder, and someone else is building on it. But each one should build with care. For no one can lay any foundation other than the one already laid, which is Jesus Christ. If anyone builds on this foundation using gold, silver, costly stones, wood, hay or straw, their work will be shown for what it is, because the Day will bring it to light. It will be revealed with fire, and the fire will test the quality of each person's work. If what has been built survives, the builder will receive a reward. If it is burned up, the builder will suffer loss but yet will be saved—even though only as one escaping through the flames. (1 Cor. 3:10–15)

He thought back on his life, how selfishly and foolishly he had lived during most of his days, how cavalier he had been about the afterlife, hardly giving it a thought. It all seemed so crazy in hindsight. Eternity is forever, and yet he was somehow able to keep his focus mostly on nonessential earthly things, like preparing for college, preparing for his career, and later preparing for retirement. He had prepared for everything but death. All the wasted time on entertaining himself, on storing up money and possessions, with no consideration for God's desire for his life . . . and when he did make time to pray, it was always for the sake of asking God to bless his agenda and all those trivial human affairs in which he was anxiously fighting to get ahead, to win arguments and competitions. All of those were inconsequential now.

> *Eternity is forever, and yet he was somehow able to keep his focus mostly on nonessential earthly things.*

He thought back to how he prepared for tests in school and how the grading at the end of the semester was never a surprise. Every student knew they were going to receive a grade and it would be based on how well they performed. So how was it he stood here now, at the end of his earthly life (actually outside of his earthly life), caught off guard by the grading system established and carried out by his Creator? How could he be caught off guard by the most important grade of all—a grade based on how well he had lived his life in light of the kingdom, the suffering, the lost, the least, the church?

He wanted to blame the church. He wanted to blame his parents. He wanted to blame *someone* for not informing him more, preparing him more. But they were not here to blame. He felt so alone. He was simply not prepared as he stood before Christ. He stood without excuse. He was speechless, for he saw Christ in all his glory and beauty. The time came, and his works were laid at his feet. He couldn't look down. Surely they were a pathetic array of mostly worthless gestures. The things he valued so highly, he now realized, were detestable to God (Luke 16:15). He wanted to relive his life. Acts of service were the gold currency here. Generosity was paying forward to this after-earth life. Hidden gestures of faith—prayer, fasting, showing love and mercy, forgiving, caring for the needy—were of eternal importance. Proclaiming his faith publicly and sharing the good news with lost souls was a mission worthy of rewards—and not just any rewards, but rewards that would never be taken away, lose their value, or fade. Rewards that would yield a harvest again and again throughout eternity.

There he stood before Christ and the great cloud of witnesses. Someone approached with a blazing torch and lowered it to the pile at his feet. The flames engulfed it, and when the smoke cleared, he was ashamed of what was left. Tears streamed down his face. The crowd that had been in complete silence was now a symphony of sorrow and weeping for his loss, his eternal position, and for those souls he had been called to on earth but ignored. He was entering into his heavenly home, void of reward, spiritually impoverished yet saved. Jesus wiped away his tears (Rev. 21:4).

> The builder will suffer loss but yet will be saved—
> even though only as one escaping through the flames.
> (1 Cor. 3:15)

William Booth, founder of the Salvation Army, once had a vision in which he died and was ushered into heaven. He had encounters with others who had passed away and had left behind close friends and relatives, people Booth was in contact with before his death. They anxiously questioned him regarding their loved ones' statuses and whether he had the opportunity to share the good news with them. Each one went away sad, for Booth was too preoccupied in his own affairs to have anything to report; while he knew Christ, he was not living fully for Christ. He eventually met Jesus face-to-face in the vision and was allowed to return to earth. After he awoke, Booth gave himself fully to Christ, who led him to found the Salvation Army. I imagine when he died in 1912, he was able to point to an army of souls who were in heaven because of sacrifices he made.

I end this reflection with an excerpt from Booth's vision as he faced his Lord's gaze, having not lived for him.

> What a look it was! It was not pain, and yet it was not
> pleasure. It was not anger, and yet it was not approval.
> Anyway, I felt that in that face, so inexpressibly admirable and glorious, there was yet no welcome for

me. I had felt this in the faces of my previous visitors. I felt it again in the Lord's.

That face, that Divine face, seemed to say to me, for language was not needed to convey to the very depths of my soul what His feelings were to me: "Thou wilt feel thyself little in harmony with these, once the companions of My tribulations and now of My glory, who counted not their lives dear unto themselves, in order that they might bring honor to Me and salvation to men." And He gave a look of admiration at the host of apostles and martyrs and warriors gathered around Him.

Oh, that look of Jesus! I felt that to have one such loving recognition—it would be worth dying a hundred deaths at the stake. It would be worth being torn asunder by wild beasts. The angelic escort felt it, too, for their responsive burst of praise and song shook the very skies and the ground on which I lay.

—excerpt from *This Was Your Life* by Rick Howard and Jamie Lash

28

#Blessed?

Prayers for God's blessing seemed to have landed me a great job, which led to my ability to purchase a beautiful home and lease a late-model car. I was gaining in so many ways and felt the favor of the Lord was upon me. For so long, I thought this was how God poured out his blessings. But was I looking through the lens of modern, Western Christianity, where many believe God favors us through material prosperity? Had I become conditioned to affluence and the belief material wealth meant, by default, God was condoning, and perhaps even promoting, this lifestyle? In American culture today, *blessing* is used to mean something more along the lines of *bliss*, to experience being made happy, prosperous, or fortunate.

> *In American culture today*, blessing *is used to mean something more along the lines of* bliss, *to experience being made happy, prosperous, or fortunate.*

Yes, all good things are from God. Perceived blessings in the form of affluence, however, may have nothing to do with you or with God condoning a lifestyle. Scripture confirms that God blesses—if we are using that term to mean "brings prosperity to"—the good and bad alike. Matthew 5:45 tells us he causes the "sun to rise on the evil and the good, and sends rain on the righteous and the unrighteous."

So then, if an evil person receives the warmth of the sun, are we to assume God is blessing that person? Yes, in the sense all good things come from God. But no, in the sense he is not specifically blessing that individual or condoning their lifestyle.

Then, are blessings benign? Or *should* blessings be benign to us? I believe they should be, because we clearly see the favor of God upon people of little means, including God's own Son. Jesus was homeless and poor throughout his ministry. Many of the disciples gave their material possessions away and lived in dependence upon God for their provisions. They did this as a guard, a hedge of protection. Funny that modern Americans are so bent on having enough money to be secure, while the disciples of Jesus chose less money to find full security in God. They had important work to do, and the distraction and potential dangers of money were not worth it to them. First Timothy 6:10 states that the love of money is the root of all kinds of evil. For the disciples, not having money helped keep them from succumbing to the temptations of self-reliance and self-sufficiency, twin evils that put self ahead of God.

The disciples chose to live in this way. They intentionally lived with less in the present in order to gain more in the eternal. Jesus, though he was rich, became poor for us so we would become eternally rich through his poverty (2 Cor. 8:9). He lived completely dependent on his Father in everything he did, and he taught this way of life to his disciples by the way he lived. Matthew 17:27 states, "But so that we may not cause offense, go to the lake and throw out your line. Take the first fish you catch; open its mouth and you will find a four-drachma coin. Take it and give it to them for my tax and yours." Even in paying taxes, Jesus brings his disciples into the work of a miracle that is more about teaching that all provision comes from God than about the tax laws themselves. The disciples lived a B-less life—a life without a Plan B. Plan A was complete trust in God's provision, and Plan B was discarded. They needed to be all in for this life of faith. Plan A would only work if Plan B was not a consideration. As I have gone through life, I have seen many people succeed, good and bad alike. Some seriously bad people have flourished the most. I believe this is due to their focus on themselves, often leading to alteration of the rules. For them, caring for a neighbor is stealing time from themselves. I'm reminded of King David's laments in Psalm 37:35: "I have seen a wicked and ruthless man flourishing like a luxuriant native tree."

We need a scriptural lens through which to rightly view so-called blessings. If material blessings are always indicators of God's favor, the wicked would be impoverished and the righteous would be rich. But the New Testament flips this on its head. We read a parable of Christ's depicting a materially blessed man walking past a desperately poor and lame beggar who was lying by his gate. In the end it was the poor man who was rich toward God yet without material gain. The wealthy man was impoverished spiritually yet had untold material wealth (Luke 16:19–26).

While it is true that not all who are financially wealthy are spiritually impoverished, and not all who are financially poor are spiritually rich, the New Testament contains many warnings for the well off and many instructions for the use of wealth. It contains almost no instructions, however, to spend on oneself or to accumulate earthly possessions. On the contrary, we have difficult prompts like these from Jesus:

> To a rich man: "If you want to be perfect, go, sell your possessions and give to the poor, and you will have treasure in heaven. Then come, follow me." (Matt. 19:21)

To his disciples: "Sell your possessions and give to the poor. Provide purses for yourselves that will not wear out, a treasure in heaven that will never fail, where no thief comes near and no moth destroys." (Luke 12:33)

To the Pharisees: "Be generous to the poor, and everything will be clean for you." (Luke 11:41)

Jesus did not just teach this way; he lived it. Out of all who have ever lived or ever will live, he gave up the most. He sacrificed unbroken fellowship with his Father and the Holy Spirit in the glory of heaven. The greatest earthly luxury would amount to nothing in comparison, and yet he chose to live a life of the less and least from earthly standards. This serves as an example that our cultural understanding of God's blessing as meaning "experiencing material abundance" is not necessarily in line with Scripture. Biblically, material abundance is not a sign of God's favor; rather, it tends to be benign. But when you have wealth and are trying to figure out what to do with it, well, that's a whole different story. If you have material privilege, spend it—wisely!

29

Cardboard People

You can judge the character of a man
by how he treats those who can do nothing for him.
−AUTHOR UNKNOWN−

Sure, I saw him lying there. Why I didn't have empathy or com-passion toward him, I really couldn't tell you. Perhaps I would have if I had stopped myself, for even a moment, to reflect on this man's plight instead of my own agenda. Nevertheless, he was an annoyance. Never missing a day, his friends faithfully dropped him off by my gate every single morning. And the dogs—oh, the dogs he would attract! Not only did I have to deal with his begging as I passed through my own gates, but those darn dogs would gather around me and my servants as we walked into the market. They were as emaciated as Lazarus. Feed them and we'd never get rid of them either. I would cringe when they came near us, such disgusting animals, licking Lazarus's sores for hours on end. Lazarus didn't seem to mind, though. Maybe the companionship of wild dogs was better than no companionship at all for a pathetic, crippled beggar.

One morning, I said to Lazarus, "Why can't you lay in front of someone else's gate for a change?"

His responses were always so gentle.

"Have mercy on me, kind sir. I don't mean to be a bother. Could you spare some food? Even if you can't, I pray for God's blessing on you and your household."

I would laugh to myself. He ought to have been praying for some kind of blessing on himself, because it was pretty clear which one of us God was blessing.

Was he crippled from birth, or did something happen to him? I never thought to ask him; actually, I ignored him most of the time. In fact, the only times I spoke to him were to tell him off or to beg him to lie in front of someone else's place. Thinking back on it now, this poor, crippled, pitiful man was the only thing in my life that really bothered or annoyed me. Once inside the walls of my dwelling, I could shut him out of my mind the way I shut him out of my gates. I even warned my servants never to feed him. If he never got any food, he might decide to lie somewhere else—or perhaps die, which (as bad as it sounds) seemed humane to me.

I wasn't naïve, though. Some of my servants were throwing scraps over the wall. As I would walk along the patio in the early evenings, sometimes I could hear the dogs fighting over the food. I doubt Lazarus got any. I thought I was being merciful by not firing my servants for it. I actually thought that was what mercy looked like.

So where did I get my frame of reference for how I lived life? My worldview came from the synagogue, of course. One would think it might be a place where a man's conscience would awaken; just the opposite, as it turned out. At the synagogue, I was released from weak, lingering guilt that may have crept in during the week. It was there I learned Lazarus was in his situation because of his sin and perhaps the sin of his parents. Me, on the other hand? God was blessing me beyond measure, as evidenced by having the best seat at the table and in the place of worship and by the overflow of my riches, which surely gave proof of God's blessing on me.

Every now and then I did wonder whether I was honored and respected only because of my wealth. After all, the Pharisees loved money just as much as I did, and I was a significant revenue stream for them. Were the messages they were serving up strategically skewed? It never occurred to me to look into my faith any further than what they were preaching. Why would I? These were men of God, after all. It just so happened that their doctrine fully supported and affirmed my selfish, lavish life. How else could I have been so heartless toward Lazarus, day in and day out, feeling so justified in the process? Why it had never occurred to me the religious could be corrupt, I cannot tell you. I guess I was blind to my own corruption. Honestly, we were all corrupt and blind, feeding on each other when we should have been feeding the poor, or at least poor Lazarus.

Truth be told, I knew, deep down, it was wrong. It is impossible to live in luxury with extreme poverty just outside your gates and not know something is wrong. But I had become so callous and caught up in the lifestyle as well as the praise of men. It was so intoxicating to be seen as important and worthy of honor. Even poor, crippled Lazarus would praise me while he begged me for scraps. I had become my own delusional god, receiving praise I did not deserve from shallow men with evil intentions—the exception, of course, being Lazarus.

It is impossible to live in luxury with extreme poverty just outside your gates and not know something is wrong.

I will never forget the day I walked out of the gate, fully expecting to hear the regular plea for food but instead hearing a swarm of flies and the chewing of dogs on his corpse. I glanced over, and my first thought was not that this poor man had died in such an undignified way; rather, it was to command my servants to clean up the mess and dispose of the body. Finally, I could go to and from my own home without being harassed for food and chased by dogs. My one and only annoyance was finally gone. How had I become so hardhearted?

"There was a rich man who was dressed in purple and fine linen and lived in luxury every day. At his gate was laid a beggar named Lazarus, covered with sores and longing to eat what fell from the rich man's table. Even the dogs came and licked his sores. The time came when the beggar died and the angels carried him to Abraham's side." (Luke 16:19–22)

Lord Jesus, help me to keep the end in mind throughout each of my days. Keep me from self-delusions and from those who would affirm these delusions that cause me to turn away from the very souls you have called me to serve, rescue, and protect. Soften my heart and open my time, my money, and my talents to respond with compassion rather than annoyance to those who live in poverty—poverty of all forms. And save me from the worst poverty of all: poverty of the soul. Empty me of my selfishness, fill me afresh with your Spirit, and give me clear actions to take today. Amen.

30

Dismissed Value

"The rich exist for the sake of the poor.
The poor exist for the salvation of the rich."

−ST. JOHN CHRYSOSTOM−

I woke to the familiar sensation of a wild dog's tongue against my sores. How I managed to sleep on the hard ground and canvas mat was a mystery to me, but I was grateful for the reprieve, however brief. Each day was the same, a fight for survival. I wasn't sure where my desire to survive came from, but it was certainly not from any future hope in this life. From all perspectives, my life was bleak and dark. Crippled at birth, rejected by my own family, and without any dignified means to provide for myself, this was who I was: rejected, an outcast.

I used to believe I had no value, that I was a waste of a life. And if the pain of being rejected by almost everyone wasn't bad enough, the physical pain of my condition served to double my afflictions.

They were still far off, but I could hear them coming, him and his entourage. My life had sunk so low that hunger was a merciful distraction, a sensation that reminded me I was alive and wanted to continue living. As disabled, afflicted, and shunned as I was, my body still fought to live, and I sought to oblige it with the slim hope of scraps from his table.

The gate was opening, and I strained to lift my head. "Please, kind sir, can you spare just some scraps?" He heard me but did not look my way—he never did—as if not acknowledging me would nullify my existence. I used to well up with anger toward him, but no longer; my anger had turned to pity. Yes, pity. I pitied this man who had lost his way and lost touch with humanity. The rejection of just one life here was a rejection of God, the Creator of all humanity. How did I know this? God came near to me. He heard me when no one else would or could. I cried out to him in my desperation and was comforted. I received what he offered me: a new life, a life not of this world; and a new spirit, his Spirit. Mine was a rebirth hidden to the self-sufficient but plain as day to the suffering, to those who have nothing. My circumstances didn't change, but I did. And, as crazy as it sounds, I wouldn't have traded places with him for all his worldly wealth, because it would have been in exchange for spiritual impoverishment. No, I was not the one to be pitied, and I knew it. I did not receive this perspective through my human understanding. This was spiritually discerned, a gift from God freely given to lowly castaways like me who need only to look up, cry out, and believe. I had this treasure within me that trumped all the wealth of the rich. But they couldn't see it, so blinded by the material, so intoxicated by power, such lovers of false praise.

The day finally came when I was at my weakest moment physically yet my strongest spiritually. My time was nearing an end. I was alone, yet I could sense angels surrounding me as I moved between agony and ecstasy nearly simultaneously. My spirit was pulling away from my body. And then, finally: release. I was free. Free from the bondage of my body, free from the pain, and free from all rejection. As my spirit lifted, I glanced down and saw the dogs now having their way with the carcass I no longer possessed. And there were the walls surrounding the massive structural kingdom of the man I had appealed to in hopes of relieving my physical hunger. I prayed for his soul one

Little did he know I was a life laid at his gate to show him the way to God, if only he'd had eyes to see it.

last time, this man who had ignored me to his own peril. Little did he know I was a life laid at his gate to show him the way to God, if only he'd had eyes to see it. If only his eyes could have been freed from the cataracts of the world.

Perhaps my death will awaken him. Perhaps my story, shared by my Savior, will serve to awaken many.

> "There was a rich man who was dressed in purple and fine linen and lived in luxury every day. At his gate was laid a beggar named Lazarus, covered with sores and longing to eat what fell from the rich man's table. Even the dogs came and licked his sores. The time came when the beggar died and the angels carried him to Abraham's side. The rich man also died and was buried." (Luke 16:19–22)

The same week as I was reflecting on this passage, the Lord gave me the opportunity to assist someone in need, a man in poverty whom I had come alongside and gotten to know throughout the past year. Honestly, this man was difficult to help; his poor choices had become perpetual, and his requests seemed never ending. Tragedy struck his life again, and he found himself homeless and helpless. This passage came alive to me, crying out to me, "This man is Lazarus lying at your gate." It was a privilege to step in and assist him in a tangible way and hard at the same time, as I often find reasons to justify a *no*. And with this individual, there were plenty. Yet God spoke to me, highlighting the unmerited grace he has lavished on me. I was so thankful I was able to "see" this man and his plight afresh and I was able to respond with resources (from above). Oh, to live this way always—and oh, how many like Lazarus I have walked by without a thought.

Lord, you have each Lazarus in your sight, in your care. Awaken me and open me to see what you see, to respond as you would have me respond. I am your servant, your ambassador. I am not my own, and I am thankful for that truth. Amen.

31

The Final Dialogue

Two very different lives are on display in Luke 16, one seemingly rich and one seemingly poor. Two lives lived at opposite ends of a wide spectrum. Two lives that intersected. And in death, two very different realities.

LAZARUS (L): I could see him off in the distance.

RICH MAN (R): I could see him off in the distance.

L: I am comforted now. I was healed and made whole.

R: I am in agony now, burning in such pain.

L: As I stood by Father Abraham, I heard the man's appeal, asking whether I might come to him to relieve his pain with a small gesture, a drop of water for his tongue. Even after all those years that he was unwilling to show compassion or pity toward me, I desperately wanted to help him. But this wasn't my choice to make.

R: I was appealing to Father Abraham, asking if he could send Lazarus to dip his finger in water and relieve my greatest pain, my burning tongue. How I wished I could have used this tongue to send servants to take Lazarus in and to relieve *his* pain during my life, or even simply to acknowledge him.

L: I heard Father Abraham's reply to his question. "Son, remember that in your lifetime you received 'good things,' while Lazarus received 'bad things,' but now he is comforted here and you are in agony. And besides all this, between us and you a great chasm has been set in place, so that those who want to go from here to you cannot, nor can anyone cross over from there to us." I was silent during the entire exchange, just as he was silent during my life. He silenced me by refusing to acknowledge me or comfort me.

R: The Lord's reply further sickened me. As selfish as I was, I thought of my brothers and said, "Then I beg you, father, send Lazarus to my family, for I have five brothers. Let him warn them, so they will not also come to this place of torment."

L: I remember his brothers. Not one of them was any different from him. I was not surprised by Father Abraham's reply: "They have Moses and the Prophets; let them listen to them."

R: "No!" I shouted. "If someone from the dead goes to them, they will repent." Surely this would be true. Who could reject the way of salvation in the face of a miracle, a man rising from the dead?

L: I heard Father Abraham's reply: "If they do not listen to Moses and the Prophets, they will not be convinced even if someone rises from the dead." How desperately blind and calloused a man must become in order to reject God even in the face of a resurrection. I felt such sorrow for the souls of all men who reject God by rejecting the neighbor at their gate.

> "I was hungry and you gave me something
> to eat, I was thirsty and you gave me
> something to drink, I was a stranger and
> you invited me in." (Matt. 25:35)

32

Heart Revealer

Disquieting care is the common fruit of an abundance of this world, and the common fault of those that have abundance. The more men have, the more perplexity they have with it.

−MATTHEW HENRY−

"Watch out!" This is how Jesus prefaces his parable on greed. He goes on to say, "Be on your guard against all kinds of greed; life does not consist in an abundance of possessions" (Luke 12:15).

When I reflect on Jesus's exclamation—"Watch out!"—it's unnerving. I imagine him raising his voice to quiet the crowd as he moves into an extremely important life lesson. He could have just warned them about greed, but he doesn't. He wants us to understand what this means within the context of a story, so we can imagine it as it relates to our lives.

And he told them this parable: "The ground of a certain rich man yielded an abundant harvest. He thought to himself, 'What shall I do? I have no place to store my crops.'

> "Then he said, 'This is what I'll do. I will tear down my barns and build bigger ones, and there I will store my surplus grain. And I'll say to myself, "You have plenty of grain laid up for many years. Take life easy; eat, drink, and be merry."'
>
> "But God said to him, 'You fool! This very night your life will be demanded from you. Then who will get what you have prepared for yourself?'
>
> "This is how it will be with whoever stores up things for themselves but is not rich toward God."
> (Luke 12:16–21)

I used to think this parable had a wealth loophole, so to speak—storing up is fine as long as you are rich toward God. The abundance of the rich man's surplus added color to the story but certainly did not seem central to the point Jesus was making. The point of this parable, I thought, was the warning to never be found impoverished in your relationship with God. After all, Jesus says, "This is how it will be with whoever stores up things for themselves but is not rich toward God." The only thing that needed adjusting was this man's relationship with God, right?

One could certainly view it this way; build up, store up, stock up, and be merry. So long as you are rich toward God, it's all good. Again, the only problem with this man was he simply wasn't rich toward God. But given that Jesus didn't speak extemporaneously and always had a basis for every detail of his parables, what was his purpose in telling the details of the crops, the surplus?

The story starts out innocent enough. A wealthy man becomes even wealthier when his crops yield an abundant harvest. This seems like a nice problem to have. He has too much and not enough room for it all. His solution is a logical and practical one: create additional room for the surplus by tearing down the existing structures and building up bigger barns. It's oddly reminiscent of the multibillion dollar storage industry in all its many forms that have popped up across the US landscape—more than 2.3 billion square feet of self-storage, a land area equivalent to three times the size of Manhattan. This man's behavior is also reminiscent of many Americans' retirement goals: work hard, invest well, and store up for the singular purpose of relaxing, taking life easy, and spending on yourself.

I now understand surplus is a revealer of a person's character. It shows where their heart is. Is this why Jesus includes this detail? Notice how the already wealthy man immediately pivots to forecasting his years of ease whereby his plans all center on one theme—himself and his pleasure. "You have plenty of grain laid up for many years. Take life easy; eat, drink, and be merry." No sooner does he get these words out than God speaks: "You fool!"

Contrast this to the statement made by wealthy Zacchaeus when he is confronted by Jesus. "Look, Lord! Here and now I give half of my possessions to the poor. . . ." As soon as he gets these words out, Jesus declares, "Today salvation has come to this house" (Luke 19:8–9).

I suspect the wealthy man in the Luke 12 story had many years to build his wealth, along with many opportunities to establish and grow his relationship with God. Yet in the end, the man was only materially rich and not rich toward God. It took one banner crop to expose his heart condition. Imagine: if he had been rich toward God, what might he have done with his surplus? Perhaps the reason he wasn't rich toward God in the first place was throughout his life he chose to expend his effort on becoming materially rich. Perhaps he felt he had earned his wealth all on his own merit, without any help from God.

Clearly the rich man cared more for his wealth than he did for his relationship with God. So much so that his immediate reaction to additional abundance was to protect it, to save it for himself rather than share it with others. In fact, he gave no thought whatsoever to others.

In our society, monetary success is held in high esteem and almost never questioned; in fact, it is often held up as greatness. Jesus reminds us here that monetary success does not equal security, nor is it an indicator of God's favor. This is why Jesus issues a stern warning that begins with "Watch out!" and is followed by a warning to guard against all kinds of greed. Greed can so easily be masked to look good and can be justified with sincere yet flawed intentions. We need to check our motives, set up guards, and not assume Jesus is referring to others rather than to us (to me). Especially given the many forms greed can take, we should "guard against all kinds of greed" (Luke 12:15).

Monetary success does not equal security, nor is it an indicator of God's favor.

In a conversation with my pastor on the topic of greed, I was honest with him about my own struggle with greed and my concern of being or becoming greedy. Pastor Brian asked me what I was doing to guard myself. I shared with him my belief that care for neighbor breaks the bonds of greed. To be with, care for, and give to the marginalized seems to be the best remedy for my self-absorbed, self-centered, greedy tendencies. Looking into the eyes of prisoners, a poor child, or someone who is hungry helps push out greed in all its forms.

Lord, thank you for your warnings and for speaking truth, truth that is hard for me to receive. I am challenged by your parable of this rich man. I see glimpses of myself in him. I'm thankful for the reminder that true riches are found only in my relationship with you. Help me to seek you first. Help me to be content with my daily bread and to desire you and your will far more than I desire earthly, temporal gain. Lead me to desire what you desire for my possessions. May my response to abundance reflect you and a concern for others and not solely myself, my happiness, and my security. Amen.

33

God or Money?

"Wow, those were some evil, egocentric, and greedy dudes!"

Have you ever scoffed at the evil, money-loving Pharisees (Luke 16:14)? I certainly have. Conveniently, I have never projected myself into the text as one of them. Perhaps the reason I haven't seen myself as one of them is evidence I am more like them than not. Clearly, they did not see themselves as evil. Scripture is explicit they were blind and self-deceived. They highly valued money and rejected the concepts they were simply managers of God's wealth and God is to be valued above all. Yet when our guard is down, we all tend to love the gift disproportionately more than we love the giver.

Earlier in Jesus's conversation with the self-deceived Pharisees, he addressed God and money head-on. He laid out the most uncomfortable contrast of hate and love between the two. Whichever one you love, by default you will hate the other. This is not a message lovers of money would welcome. But because it was true, Jesus spoke it plainly: "No one can serve two masters.

Either you will hate the one and love the other, or you will be devoted to the one and despise the other. You cannot serve both God and money" (Luke 16:13). The Pharisees loved money, and, at the same time, they loved being seen as godly. They nailed the outward actions as they tithed their money, studied Scripture,

As wealth loses its grip on us, we become free to love God and carry out his mission as he intended.

and practiced the law and all its attendant rituals. All of these behaviors were intentionally visible to the public, yet somehow their love of money and service to money became the target of Jesus's scorn. Perhaps all their public practices and added rules allowed them to put on a facade of righteousness in order simply to amass more money.

Somewhere along the way, money became their God and their master. Jesus publicly unmasked their intentions, and without any trace of ambiguity. "You cannot serve both God and money," he stated. He stepped it up even further to say that their love for money caused them to despise God.

Is this why Jesus was so quick to instruct his listeners to give without reservation to the poor? Is this why most of his teachings on money end with him telling his listeners to give rather than acquire? Try to find Jesus speaking anywhere on worldly accumulation or acquisition. In addition to the indwelling of his Spirit, it was the disciples' putting into practice Jesus's teaching on money that allowed them to follow him with such resolute devotion to his mission. They couldn't be bought, nor could they be distracted by earthly aggregation. Worldly wealth simply had no appeal. Having little made it easier for them to see over the horizon to heaven, the place God has ordained for us to accumulate lasting wealth (Luke 12:33).

As wealth loses its grip on us, we become free to love God and carry out his mission as he intended. And as Jesus points out, a growing love for God means a growing abhorrence of money.

Unfortunately, our Western culture conditions us to love money (possessions, wealth, security, etc.), while the New Testament stands as a signpost pointing in exactly the opposite direction.

Far too often our churches are shaped and influenced by culture, rather than the other way around. Money is required to cover the overhead, which can lead to a compromised, watered-down gospel, one that panders to the masses. Some churches that preach Jesus's words may face the "Jesus effect"—the emptying of their pews (John 6:66). Pastors today can find themselves in this pickle, tempted to give their congregants what they desire to hear and not what they need to hear. When this occurs, congregants can become like spoiled children who refuse to eat healthy food and demand only junk food. If we're not careful, the church can be the place we go to justify, not modify, our lives (2 Tim. 4:3).

We must hate, despise, or detest money rather than love, serve, or devote ourselves to it. These strongly contrasting verbs—*hate, despise, detest* vs. *love, serve, devote*—are words our Savior uses to bring reality into view regarding money and God. Regardless of our desire to love both, only one will emerge preeminent. It is shocking to think we could become haters or despisers of God because of our love for and devotion to money. This word of warning seems counter to modern teaching, and it is often simply ignored. But the love of money, Scripture tells us, is a root of all kinds of evil (1 Tim. 6:10), the worst of which is to love it and despise God.

Truth be told, I want to align myself with both God and money. Sadly, I would receive little pushback from those in our culture if I loved money and appeared to also love God. This is why hearing directly from Jesus and meditating on his words is so crucial. Thankfully, Jesus has no problem calling me out.

I see wealth all around me, and alongside it I see great admiration for those who hold it. I encountered the überwealthy just last night at a local restaurant, in fact. Their vehicle drove up and their security guards ushered them in. The vehicle remained running the entire time they were at the restaurant—presumably to ensure the perfect internal temperature when they got back in. This may seem small, but it is indicative of an overarching privileged position they hold. Because they can, they will, and they do, which creates an extreme separation from the common person.

Sometimes I try to envision what it will be like on the other side of the grave. Jesus made it clear that "many who are first will be last, and the last first" (Mark 10:31). I wonder about those living a life of privilege now, myself included. Do we realize how low we may find ourselves in eternity? Do we have awareness of Jesus's teaching? Are we seeking to be first? Can we find God while we are surrounded by luxury, which so often separates us from neighbors in need?

We see great poverty and need all around us, a growing gap between rich and poor, and injustices that must weigh heavy on our Lord. Jesus expressed his emotions against the injustices of his day. I can't fathom how he feels now.

Amidst it all, I'm thankful God is a God of grace and mercy. He is patient with me. Apart from him doing his work in me through his Word and his Spirit, I am helpless in my quest to have my love for him be preeminent. Yes, I'm thankful he is working to free me from the traps of possessions and position as I open myself more and more to Christ's love that is always at work in me.

34

Parachute People

They boarded the plane with the best of intentions. Boarding had not been optional. The trip was straightforward enough. They all knew the final destination of the flight. But they also knew the plane was flawed and was destined to crash. A lifesaving provision had been prepared for each one of them. Yet the clarity they had possessed during the preflight instructions waned once airborne. For many, following the instructions was complicated by pesky distractions that pulled them away from what ultimately was in their best interest.

A parachute had been perfectly fitted for each person on board. The jump was the whole point. The jump was the alternate destination, and the parachute was their safety provision. The leap required faith in the chute, and the chute was their only hope for making it down alive.

The parachute rigs had been strategically placed at access points throughout the plane. They served as reminders of their mission—a lifesaving mission. But it was not easy to leave the comfort of the plane for the unknown elements. It was far easier, albeit deadly, for the passengers to put off the jump for another day, and then another. Tomorrow always seemed like a better time to exit the plane.

Although the future crash was a surety, the timing was unknown. Still, there was no denying it. In fact, of all the varied viewpoints and beliefs held by the passengers, the one to which they all agreed was the certainty of the crash.

The behavior of some of the passengers (not all, but many) was odd at times. They seemed to live within a trance of distraction. They acted in ways that ran counter to the reality of their circumstance. It was not that they were crazy, yet crazy is a fitting word for their reckless passivity in not acting swiftly to avoid the certainty of their fate. Did they not realize inaction is an active choice? How could they be so relaxed? How could they laugh, soak in entertainment, eat, drink, and be merry in the face of what lay ahead?

Alas, another agenda was at play, a sinister one: evil in disguise. Powers were preying on the people who were unaware. Using whatever means were available, they sought to distract the passengers from their mission. They kept their cups full of drink, their minds full of gossip and song, and their bellies full of the richest foods. They resented the passengers for their access to an escape—an option they themselves no longer had. This evil in disguise desired the passengers to share their same fate: self-destruction.

They jumped because they knew they had been called to jump.

Another force was also at work: a force for good. This force would whisper to the passengers to jump, to save their souls, to not buy into the pleasures of the plane, to sacrifice now, to risk the elements, and to live into their call to jump. Seldom was the whisper heard over the noise, the headphones, the laughter, or the passengers' inebriated state.

On occasion, a passenger would become a parachutist and jump. Putting their trust in the chute and its ability to save them, they jumped without the knowledge of exactly where they might land or what they would find. They jumped because they knew they had been called to jump. And in the jumping, they knew they would be saved from the certainty of death.

The last group of passengers, the craziest of all, were the pack people. They were the passengers who knew everything there was to know about the chutes. They would gather in packs, always with their parachute rigs properly fastened and displayed for the other passengers to see. They would recite the parachute operation and activation instructions to each other and perform prejump gear checks. But the evil powers had convinced them it was enough simply to be prepared. They never jumped.

> "You study the Scriptures diligently because
> you think that in them you have eternal life. These
> are the very Scriptures that testify about me, yet
> you refuse to come to me [jump] to have life."
> (John 5:39–40)

> In the same way, faith by itself, if it is not
> accompanied by action [jumping], is dead. (James 2:17)

> "Very truly I tell you, unless a kernel of wheat falls
> to the ground and dies [jumps], it remains only a
> single seed. But if it dies, it produces many seeds.
> Anyone who loves their life will lose it, while
> anyone who hates their life in this world [the plane]
> will keep it for eternal life." (John 12:24–25)

35

The Storm of a Lifetime

I looked out at the audience of men who had gathered for the Bible study I was leading at a church in Green Bay. Referencing Luke 6:46–49, I spoke words I thought were for them but ended up being just as much for me: "A storm is coming; it's not if, but when. The real question is, are you prepared? Only in the storm does your true character reveal itself. Will you be able to weather it because of where you have placed yourself? Or will you collapse?"

Only in the storm does your true character reveal itself.

The next day I lost my job.

SEPTEMBER 10, 2002

I sat directly across from the owner and president at our Design Priority Committee, or DPC, as we called it. A high-level meeting with key department heads, held in the corporate boardroom, where new projects were pitched and active-development projects were reviewed and signed off on by upper management.

I was vice president of design for this Fortune 1000 company, and DPC was a meeting I led. After seven years with the company, I was somewhat comfortable with my role, but this job was not for the faint of heart. I put my all into it, traveling across the US and Europe to meet with clients, attend shows, and conduct research for new products. When I wasn't traveling, I was in the office managing my staff, directing meetings, and ideating on new concepts. Stress came with this job. In fact, I had a large bottle of Excedrin at my desk that I dipped into daily to keep the pounding headaches at bay.

The meeting was rolling along as usual. I didn't see our CFO enter the room, but I looked up from my notes when I heard his voice asking if he could see me for a moment. Quickly agreeing, I couldn't help thinking how weird it was to be pulled out of a meeting with the president, especially a meeting I was leading. This must be important. I swiftly followed him out and into the corporate conference room just down the hall.

As we were sitting down, he introduced me to the only other person in the room, a paralegal from a law firm. There were large stacks of paper on the table. The CFO jumped right to his agenda.

"I understand you're involved with selling vitamins."

I responded with a yes in a rather cavalier tone. What was the big deal? When was he going to get to the point so I could get back to my meeting?

The CFO, stoic by nature, was more stoic than usual as he continued. "We take this very seriously." I was still clueless as to where this was going. "This is illegal."

At this point, I pushed back. "What are you talking about?" I sternly added, "Careful now, it is not illegal."

"It is in a few states."

"Not this one."

Then the meeting took an unexpected turn. He was done with conversation and simply said, "This is where this is going." He pulled out a letter and set it in front of me. I glanced down at this short, one-sentence letter that had my name after the salutation. It was my resignation letter, prepared by them. He proceeded to tell me I had only two options, either sign the letter or be terminated.

I was stunned. I never saw this coming. Looking at him, my colleague, I found myself repeating his name in a soft tone, over and over, as if to ask, *Why?* and *Are you sure?* I was in utter disbelief. I asked to see the owner but was denied. I asked if I could call my wife, only to be denied again.

"You have two minutes," he said, "to sign it or be terminated." In either case, he laid out what was to happen next. "You will be escorted across campus by Beth." Beth was the human resources lead. "She will oversee the gathering of your belongings and escort you to your car."

Time stood still for me. I was in shock, yet somehow I was able to pull myself together enough to professionally address him and give him my decision. I took the pen, signed my resignation, and thanked him for allowing me to resign.

With that, he left the room to get Beth, leaving me sitting with the paralegal. To my surprise, she said, "If it's any consolation, he has lost a lot of sleep over this." I didn't respond, but I thought, *I'll bet he has.* This was unjust, and I was glad he knew it. It was a clear signal our CFO was only following orders and this decision had been handed down from the owner. Only in the following days and weeks ahead was I able to piece together the real reason.

I walked with the head of HR across campus to my office. This was going to be extra difficult because it was 2:30 in the afternoon and my office had two glass walls. Surely that was no coincidence. It wasn't enough to let me go; a little extra humiliation would go a long way. Fortunately, I wasn't worried about what my staff would think. I knew they cared about me, just as they had always known I had their backs. They had come to see a number of injustices in this company, just as I had; some of them might even be envious I was leaving.

As I sat at my desk, pulling my personal items off the shelves and gathering papers and other odds and ends, something welled up inside me I couldn't hold in. I looked my colleague, Beth, in the eye and said, "Are you kidding me? Really? You're letting me go! Me! I have given my all for this company. Let go by a man who has settled numerous court cases out of court for misconduct, and you are letting *me* go? And for what? Vitamins! Are you kidding!" She couldn't even look at me. She just stared at the ground and shook her head and said, "I know, I know." She was just following orders as well. My punishment was compounded by no severance, loss of a substantial bonus I had earned, loss of a significant percentage of my vesting (just months away from fully vested), and loss of wages during the unemployment period.

I asked to say goodbye to my staff, which she allowed, as long as she could be by my side. My staff was as stunned as I, no doubt fearing that if something like this could happen to me, it could also happen to them.

In time, I came to find out the primary reason for my dismissal had to do with a company-wide noncompete agreement I refused to sign. After nearly seven years with the firm, I found a noncompete document in my inbox—it was sent across the entire organization. Our CFO, in not-so-optional language, requested that it be signed. I read it over and felt it was unfair because it gave the organization the ability to fire employees at will and then prevent us from employment in our industry for nearly two years in exchange for a two-week severance. I sent the document to my personal attorney, who advised me not to sign it. "You're better off if they fire you now than to sign this," he said. It was well crafted and would hold up in court.

I knew this noncompete was becoming an issue for me. The owner had personally asked me to sign it more than once. One afternoon, during a one-on-one meeting with the owner, the CFO stopped by his office and the two of them pressed hard for my signature. I remember this meeting well. I recall looking at the owner and personally addressing him.

"I like you," I said, "and I like working here. But if you were to get hit by a train tomorrow and a new management team came in that I couldn't work with, I would have no choice but to stay." The CFO simply stated he would not allow that to happen. Of course, that was a shallow promise he could never deliver on. Although this was the primary reason for my dismissal, there may have been others. One that most likely put the owner over the edge was his discovery I was inquiring about an open position with a competitor. The company was a friendly competitor, so much so that we were supplying tables for one of their markets. At one point, the other company had even looked at buying ours. My administrative assistant later informed me of evidence she had that before my dismissal they had discovered I had an interview lined up with them.

I kept the interview date, which ended up being just days after my dismissal. I was anxious about questions I knew they would raise regarding my recent unemployed status. My first interview was with a senior VP, who led with this question: "How in the world did you last seven years there?" That certainly put me at ease. She was referencing the company's legendary reputation as being a tough place to work. Things became laughable when in my second interview their president inquired about the vitamins I sold, wanting to know where he could get some for himself. I came away from my interviews feeling somewhat exonerated of my recent dismissal, but it was a thin salve that wore off quickly.

In the end, I didn't get the job. More dark days were ahead.

36

The Aftermath

Nothing could have prepared me for the silence or the feelings of betrayal and loss during that time. Sitting in my living room, staring at the walls and sinking lower and lower, days turned into weeks and weeks into months. The phone hardly rang (this was before texting and social media); it was eerie. I had given so much of myself to people who didn't care deeply about me, and I had ignored those who *did* care—and who were standing with me now, especially my family. This would never happen again!

It was during this time, what I now refer to as my "forced sabbatical," that I reconnected with God in a deeper way than I had ever experienced before. Part of the reconnection process was an acknowledgement of my emotions before him. Especially early on, it felt like a never-ending roller-coaster ride, where I was being whipped around in anger, fear, confusion, and even disgrace.

Disgrace hit me hard. Having no control of my reputation was exasperating. Shortly after my dismissal, I received a call from an outside supplier, who said, "I heard you were involved in a financial pyramid scheme." I was someone who sought to be aboveboard in all my dealings. My reputation was extremely important to me, yet false accusations were swirling that could destroy a well-lived, well-intended life: mine. There was nothing I could do. The real reason for my dismissal had nothing to do with the stated reason, and now the stated reason had ballooned into a much-worse, false narrative. How does one control the spread? Especially the one who was escorted out in broad daylight? Others must have doubted my innocence: "Oh, sure, you didn't do anything deserving of punishment. Right. . . ." Word got back to me that some of my former colleagues, high-level salespeople, were pushing back on the decision, calling the owner and saying things like, "Seriously, this was worthy of a slap on the wrist at most!" I never heard how the owner responded to their pressure.

It's strange to feel disgrace for something you didn't do, or in my case for something I did do but for which the punishment clearly did not fit. Yes, I did something wrong, and I own that. But a conflict of interest in selling some vitamins seemed so benign, especially given the numerous multi-level companies other people within our company were involved with—everything from Tupperware to cleaning supplies. Ironically, had one of our regional sales VPs not stepped into my office to drop off some free vitamin samples, I would not have tried the product and recovered from a serious sinus infection. I had to keep reminding myself this was not the real reason behind my dismissal. If it were, then why did I feel like a child who'd snuck a cookie from the cookie jar and ended up being locked in the basement for weeks on end as punishment? It didn't add up. But even the absurdity of my circumstances couldn't erase or lessen the shame I felt at not being able to completely deny any culpability.

During the time of my forced sabbatical, while my wounds

were still fresh, I remained deep in solitude. I established a routine during my three months of not doing. I would wake up and go on a two-hour walk, after which I would head down into my office to read, write, and reflect. My emotions were always better in the mornings. By around 2:00 p.m. I would start to crash and feel despair overtake me. I did a lot of journaling during that time. Some of my entries were just raw and honest. Others were more thoughtful, with symbolism to describe where I was inside my head, heart, and soul.

How fascinating that God breaks through to us in our pain more than at any other time. I suppose this is when he finally has our attention to let us know how much he has missed us and how much he can relate to our pain and rejection and now we can relate a bit to his. We often forget how he was a man of sorrows, how he was rejected, and how much pain he endured to make a way for him to rescue us.

His deep love, while absent at first, broke through to me during my dark days. These were days when the painful emotions subsided enough to allow me to see and let go of all the empty stuff I had been clinging to my whole life. It was a beautiful release. I could now see that my connection to Christ was not obligatory; it was love. A deep abiding love. He was seeking me in my distress, and he found me where I could be found, in that place where he was all I had, that place where I had been stripped of everything else. He found me in my pain. He found me despite my drift away from him. He found me despite my anger at him for allowing tragedy to strike my life years earlier. He found me despite my sin, both covert and overt. Yes, I was lost, and he—the Good Shepherd, who leaves his flock to seek out the one lost lamb—was now celebrating our reestablished communion together.

> *. . . he finally has our attention to let us know how much he has missed us and how much he can relate to our pain and rejection and now we can relate a bit to his.*

37

Purpose in Suffering

Journaling was cathartic for me during my unemployment. Seeing through the lens of suffering was a strangely positive experience as it stripped away the nonessentials and allowed me to hold loosely to what remained. God came near during this time in ways I had not expected or known before.

SEPTEMBER 19, 2002

God granted me a good night's sleep. Not all the way through, but restful nonetheless. I was up in the middle of the night reading *Streams in the Desert*, a daily devotional written by Lettie Cowman that has become a Christian classic on faith during difficult times. This book was given to me by my mother-in-law, Mary, and has been a godsend. It was interesting to read the entry for September 10, the day my world broke. I was especially struck by Cowman's reference to Psalm 138:8 ESV: "The Lord will fulfill his purpose for me." The author went on to recognize that "suffering is a divine mystery with a strange and supernatural power. No one has ever developed a deep level of spirituality or holiness without experiencing a great deal of suffering."

The entire section seemed to correlate to what I experienced just nine days ago. Suffering is a process that feels like a pruning of self—self-desires along with self-preservations. If we are still and submissive to it, suffering will create a dependence on God, likely a dependence that is initially not even desired. Now I see how independent I have been, being in control, self-reliant, self-sufficient. Suffering has brought this into view. True dependence on God requires death at every level of myself, including death to my inward desires, which naturally bubble up from within me. As they surface, each one of them must be put to death in order for true dependence on God to occur.

> If we are still and submissive to it, suffering will create a dependence on God, likely a dependence that is initially not even desired.

Cowman expressed it this way:

In this condition [suffering] our entire being lies perfectly still under the hand of God: every power and ability of the mind, will, and heart are at last submissive; a quietness of eternity settles into the entire soul; and finally, the mouth becomes quiet, having only a few words to say, and stops crying out the words Christ quoted on the cross: "My God, my God, why have you forsaken me?" (Ps. 22:1). At this point the person stops imagining castles in the sky and pursuing foolish ideas, and his releasing becomes calm and relaxed, with all choices removed, because the only choice has now become the purpose of God. Also his emotions have been weaned away from other people and things, becoming deadened so that nothing can hurt, offend, hinder, or get in his way. He can now let the circumstances be what they may, and continue to seek only God and His will, with the calm assurance that He is causing everything in the universe, whether good or bad, past or present, to work "for the good of those who love him" (Rom. 8:28). Oh, the blessing of absolute submission to Christ! What a blessing to lose our own strength, wisdom, plans and desires and to be where every ounce of our being becomes like a peaceful Sea of Galilee under the feet of Jesus!

This so captures the place I find myself. These words, the events, all point to God's purpose. He is always forming a plan for ultimate good; his divine hand is forming his purpose in me. His purpose, his purpose, his purpose, oh, his glorious purpose.

> *Lord, grant me the vision to see it. Grant me the wisdom to understand it. Grant me the power to fulfill it. And grant me the humility to stay in it. Amen.*

38

Shallow Roots

My morning walks brought me into contact with God's creation, with the beauty and intricacy of the natural world, which God often used to speak truth to me. Pressing through the pain of loss builds character and depth, I learned, if one is willing to suffer in the right sort of way—by letting go of anger, resentment, and frustration and by embracing the lessons.

OCTOBER 15, 2002

On my walk this morning, it caught my attention: a tree with an expansive, far-reaching, exposed root structure that, I imagined, allowed it to grow vertically with ease. From the trunk up, this tree looked like all the others—but only from the trunk up. The surrounding trees hid their roots deep beneath the surface.

Why were this tree's roots exposed? Why were they not deep within the soil like the others? Perhaps it wasn't necessary to go deep. Perhaps all it needed was provided on the surface. No need to go deep for nourishment when nourishment was effortlessly available on the surface. On the surface (pun intended), it seemed well positioned. No struggles required, just a life of ease and abundance for this fortunate tree.

On occasion I have crossed paths with individuals who are like this tree—lacking depth, born into a silver-platter existence, every need met, every desire catered to. Not only do they live a life of privilege, but they see themselves as deserving of it. I would be lying if I said I never found myself desiring that lifestyle. The things I could do, the places I could go, the businesses I could build—if only I were them. But are they really who I want to be? No, my desire is not to be like them; rather, it's to have what they have, for surely I would be a different person than they are. They are not the people I want to be, but they possess what I desire to possess.

> It is simply not possible to achieve depth without struggle.

At my core, I know it is simply not possible to achieve depth without struggle. Struggle, sacrifice, and even pain are all part of the growth process as my roots seek to push deeper into the soil. It is good for me to be reminded of this.

When I look closely at "surface people," I see a shallow life resulting from a life of ease. I see a lack of vulnerability and resiliency in those deficient in depth. A brisk wind of adversity could unravel and collapse their lives. I now understand the trade-off of what I desire to become versus what I think I want or need.

Yes, it's painful to go through pain, it hurts to hurt, and sorrow is a lonely, awful place to reside. But when I fix my mind's eye on the surface roots and all the associated shallowness, I find renewed strength to endure the painful path to depth. I find the courage to fight against the temptation to take shortcuts. I choose to allow suffering to do its deep, necessary work in my life. It is a welcome companion on my journey. I invite it in, allowing it to perform its intended, God-ordained purpose for the sake of the fruit—strength and resilience—produced by a life tried, tested, and trained by suffering.

I take comfort in these reminders:

> Consider it pure joy, my brothers and sisters,
> whenever you face trials of many kinds,
> because you know that the testing of your
> faith produces perseverance. Let perseverance
> finish its work so that you may be mature and
> complete, not lacking anything. (James 1:2–4)

> For our light and momentary troubles are
> achieving for us an eternal glory that far outweighs
> them all. So we fix our eyes not on what is seen, but
> on what is unseen, since what is seen is temporary,
> but what is unseen is eternal. (2 Cor. 4:17–18)

39

I Am Here Now

Where am I today?

I am here now: sixteen years removed from the dark days of unemployment.

During those years, we adopted our amazing daughter, Grace. We raised our boys and watched them become men. I started a few companies. Chris and I celebrated sixteen anniversaries—number thirty-two was yesterday. We welcomed our first grand-child into the world: Karleigh Jean Bakker, named after her great-grandfather Karl Bakker, my beloved father.

I am here now: far removed from my life-altering storm, and yet the experiences from that time are now part of me. I am forever changed by my suffering; it has formed me. My Lord allowed me to share in a snippet of his anguish, his pain, his rejection. I have learned lessons from suffering then, and I am learning lessons from gain now. Financial gain has proved to be the greater of the two burdens, for with it comes a responsibility demanding constant attention. There is now a relentless pull between get and give, obtain and release, mine and yours, saving and sharing.

More reflective now, I am able to make sense of life while simultaneously not having a clue. I am somehow becoming comfortable with the ambiguity of never fully knowing or controlling what lies ahead. Questions have multiplied faster than answers can be uncovered, yet I have made peace with the uncertainty. There will always be unanswered questions that beg for anxious thoughts and emotions. The only antidote for these poisons is the peace of Christ. Peace resides in the stillness of him. Nothing matters when he fully occupies us. He stills the rough waters of life. In the stillness we can see him, and in him all our questions and anxiety dissolve as he occupies us.

> *I am somehow becoming comfortable with the ambiguity of never fully knowing or controlling what lies ahead.*

> For in Christ all the fullness of the Deity lives in bodily form, and in Christ you have been brought to fullness. He is the head over every power and authority. (Col. 2:9–10)

My wonderful, awful experience of unemployment, as I think of it now, was a time of processing—processing pain, anger, injustice, and unanswered questions. And in the process, I found God.

OCTOBER 17, 2002
> Things are not as they seem; they almost never are.
> There is never just one reason, or one obvious
>   answer.
> I will never fully understand the whys.
> Life is just that way in various seasons.
> The hard part of life, to be sure.
> The painful part.

Living through this dark season, within this
    unanswerable state,
where confusion swirls around
seeking to break down all that had held me
    together.
An awful place.
Owning poor choices is part of the pain.
Accepting the severity and swiftness of this
    punishment
cuts deep into all that I consider fair and right.
It seems beyond justice and fairness,
beyond, far beyond, but nonetheless it is.
Owning it with all the consequences
brings me into a state of complete brokenness.
Yes, an awful place, but wonderful as well,
seeing life through an altogether different lens.
The view is clearer when
all that you considered "you" is pruned back
to the essence of "you."
I am not my title, my possessions, or my position.
I am not these things or even my reputation.
I am me, apart from all those things.
How clear the view is
with the nonessentials
stripped
away.
I see
the important elements of life;
I see
the pain and plight of others from the perspective
    of this new place.
I understand
that which I only thought I understood before.

Faith
is the anchor that holds me amidst the waves of
this storm.
This storm
will calm and is calming.
The sun
will shine brightly again on the horizon of my soul.
The lessons learned will be with me always.

This poem, attributed to Robert Browning Hamilton, expresses it best.

I walked a mile with Pleasure,
She chattered all the way:
But left me none the wiser
For all she had to say.
I walked a mile with Sorrow,
And ne'er a word said she;
But oh, the things I learned from her
When Sorrow walked with me.

40

The Remedy

This man, Jesus, absolutely intrigued him. All the talk around town centered on his miraculous works and how he taught with such authority. He desperately wanted to understand Jesus's intentions and gain his attention. Even now, as Jesus taught, the man hoped for a way to get time with this unusual teacher. When Jesus stopped speaking and began to walk his way, the man seized the opportunity to extend an invitation to eat lunch with him. To his surprise, Jesus accepted, came in, and immediately reclined at the table.

While Jesus relaxed, the man proceeded to the washing bowl to cleanse himself before the meal, as required by Jewish law. He did not wish to start his time with Jesus on edge, but why was Jesus not yet getting up to wash his hands! What kind of Jew was he? Didn't he realize people were watching with the expectation that we follow the law and follow it to the letter? Who was this man? People were claiming he was a great teacher and prophet, but he didn't even keep the simplest commandment?

He tried to play it cool, but Jesus could see his body language, not to mention read his thoughts. As was his way, Jesus wasted no time speaking truth without regard for the audience. "Now then, you Pharisees clean the outside of the cup and dish, but inside you are full of greed and wickedness. You foolish people! Did not the one who made the outside make the inside also? But now as for what is inside you—be generous to the poor, and everything will be clean for you" (See Luke 11:37–41).

———

I came across this section of Scripture a number of years ago. It jumped out at me in a big way, especially verse forty-one. "But now as for what is inside you—be generous to the poor, and everything will be clean for you." The rest of the passage made sense to me. After all, calling out a group of Pharisees for their hypocrisy was a regular occurrence with Jesus. But I just could not get my head around verse forty-one. It seemed so out of place. On the surface, it seemed like an error. This man and his clan, the Pharisees, were hypocrites for sure; they loved being honored and respected by the masses. They were, however, self-deceived: drinking their own Kool-Aid, creating law upon law, ritual upon ritual, to set themselves apart. They lost (or perhaps never had) a connection to God, confusing an outward, godly appearance with a genuine relationship. Jesus called it cleaning the outside of the cup without paying any attention to the greed and wickedness within.

Let's return to verse forty-one. "But now as for what is inside you—be generous to the poor, and everything will be clean for you."

But how? How is it that generosity alone could cleanse inwardly? Is he really saying (or really meaning) that if they would just open their purse strings and be generous directly to the poor it would remedy their greed and wickedness? Well, that *is* what the verse says. In the midst of a familiar story, this was an astounding revelation for me, hitting on what most of us long for: to be internally clean. My heart jumped when I read this verse the very first time, because I could identify with the Pharisee. I hid behind my weekly church attendance (washing the cup's exterior) while a genuine relationship with Christ felt dormant. Greed and wickedness lay just below the surface of my otherwise polished life. Despite my own materialism and hidden selfishness, I desperately wanted a remedy and there it was in Luke 11:41. The remedy was generosity.

What I have come to realize is that what Jesus was asking of these Pharisees was not possible, humanly speaking. A greedy person cannot be generous, especially toward the poor, without a heart change. Jesus chose to highlight the resulting effect of a heart change without mentioning the transformation itself. This is certainly not the only time Jesus called for or commended individuals for paying attention to and giving generously to the poor.

Isaiah 58:6–8 is a compelling Old Testament passage calling us to serve the poor and vulnerable, the result being light, healing, and righteousness. All will be clean for you!

> "Is not this the kind of fasting I have chosen: to loose the chains of injustice and untie the cords of the yoke, to set the oppressed free and break every yoke? Is it not to share your food with the hungry and to provide the poor wanderer with shelter— when you see the naked, to clothe them, and not to turn away from your own flesh and blood? Then your light will break forth like the dawn, and your healing will quickly appear; then your *righteousness* will go before you, and the glory of the Lord will be your rear guard." (Isa. 58:6–8)

My eyes were first opened to the poor through David Platt's book *Radical*. Shortly after reading this book I traveled to Haiti with my best friend and my second son, Joshua. This trip had a profound effect on all of our lives. Seeing the poverty of that developing country was gut-wrenching, depressing, and overwhelming. I knew I would never be the same or look at life through the same lens. Jesus stated that the poor will always be with us (John 12:8), which I now see as a gift to both ends of the socioeconomic spectrum; they are in desperate need of each other. Life unintentionally loses meaning when spent on oneself, deteriorating into emptiness and greed. The great twentieth-century American performer Jackie Gleason put it well: "When I experienced success, I said, 'I had better get all the things I've always wanted.' I mean, how fruitless to be able to afford them but not get them. I soon realized that material things are not of great value. Once I got them, they lost all their greatness."

When we open the Bible with an eye toward the poor, we quickly discover how much we need to serve the poor and need to *become* poor, so to speak. Not necessarily through actual poverty, unless God has called us to that, but certainly through proximity to the poor and through carrying burdens together. This is often through money but not always. Some may say, "I have nothing to give." We all have ways for generosity to become the remedy. One way I have done this is through teaching a weekly class in a local prison. Each week I share, but mostly I listen to stories of heartache and wisdom. I cannot give the inmates anything monetarily, yet I still choose generosity by giving of myself. And they give me hope simply by being with me.

> As we live into generosity, there is a beautiful mutuality that unfolds, a blurring of roles between giver and receiver.

As we live into generosity, there is a beautiful mutuality that unfolds, a blurring of roles between giver and receiver. Might we be receiving more than we are giving? Cleanliness through generosity; it's a peculiar prescription, but take it on a regular basis, and experience the remedy for yourself.

> Create in me a clean heart, O God; and renew
> a right spirit within me. (Ps. 51:10 KJV)

41

Shrewd

He is no fool who gives what he cannot keep

to gain what he cannot lose.

−JIM ELLIOT−

He was going about his business, handling the affairs of his employer's estate in his usual way. Rarely satisfied with or proud of himself, he knew he could do better; he knew he could be better. Unfortunately, his desire to improve was offset by the ease of cutting corners in managing Mr. Smith's assets. Who would know anyway? No one was paying attention, certainly not the trusting Mr. Smith. If it were not for the occasional pangs of his conscience, like speed bumps on an otherwise smooth road, his life would be easy street.

What he did not account for was the watchful eye of a conscientious person living in his community. He had no way of knowing who it was, but he had his suspicions. When he heard Mr. Smith's words, "What is this I hear about you? You have mismanaged my estate. Get your affairs in order. You will not be my manager much longer," he knew they were warranted, even overdue. He was being called to account for wasting Mr. Smith's possessions.

What had seemed so harmless to him, a duplicitous act here and there, now felt so much worse when called into the light. He wanted to protest, but that would only add to his already full cup of guilt and shed more light on the details of his shameful actions. He was confident his indiscretions went well beyond those brought to Mr. Smith's attention. Best to let those dogs sleep.

It was hard for him to discern whether he felt worse about his multiple indiscretions or about failing the man who had entrusted him with all his possessions. His mind raced ahead to consider his future, since salvaging his job was not even remotely possible. The grounds of his termination coupled with his lack of qualifications to do any other dignified work meant that backbreaking manual labor or begging were his only prospective options. Neither of these had any appeal—far from it.

Perhaps one last round of indiscretion was in order. He was surprised at how quickly his feelings of shame over letting Mr. Smith down vanished against his instinct for self-preservation. So again, as was his custom, he devised a shrewd plan, one that was foolproof and heart-wrenching at the same time. Heart-wrenching because it meant robbing Mr. Smith again, but this time the skimming wouldn't be subtle; it would be blatant and outright.

Time was of the essence, so while he still had access to all the accounts, he set up appointments with each of Mr. Smith's debtors. With breakneck speed, he moved through each one, officially sealing and signing off on significant debt reduction. Each debtor was surprised, delighted, and felt immediately indebted to him—his objective all along. Relieve their debt burden so they would be obligated to him. His future would surely not be as ideal as his past, but being a welcomed guest in the homes of Mr. Smith's debtors was clearly better than any alternative he could conjure in the spur of the moment.

Just as he was wrapping up his final appointment, the door swung open, and there stood Mr. Smith. The last debtor scurried out and around him like a cockroach suddenly exposed to light. Time was up; he was caught. He sheepishly looked up, and Mr. Smith snatched the debt journal from his hand to examine it.

To his surprise, with a half-smile on his lips, Mr. Smith said, "Well played!"

How could this be? Mr. Smith, whom he had let down in more ways than could be humanly counted, was now commending him for his shrewdness? Was he not losing his job because he had mismanaged and wasted Mr. Smith's possessions? How was it that his act of reducing the debts of his employer's debtors was commendable and not condemnable? Was not this last act more damaging and rapacious than all the other indiscretions combined—gaining favor and friendships using Mr. Smith's money? He could never have envisioned indirectly gaining favor from Mr. Smith as well.

Mr. Smith was gracious and refrained from giving him what he deserved. He could have easily prevented the success of his last scheme by pressing charges and throwing him in jail. Instead, he was merciful toward him, and toward his debtors as well.

This parable from Luke 16:1–8, reshaped for a modern context, came into my view many years ago and has caused me to ponder ever since. It is both strange and fascinating.

After the parable, Jesus implies we should be more shrewd in our dealings and goes on to say, "I tell you, use worldly wealth to gain friends for yourselves, so that when it is gone, you will be welcomed into eternal dwellings" (Luke 16:9). What does being welcomed into eternal dwellings mean in this context? My oldest son, David, and I were having a conversation about the meaning of this verse, and we came away believing that, on the other side, all those who we have given to and sacrificed for would be eternally grateful and indebted. Our earthly spending will bring eternal benefits, both for ourselves and for those to whom we have shown generosity.

We are all managers of a portion of our Master's (God's) possessions he has entrusted to us. Because we are sinful by nature, we are wasteful by nature. He has every right to take this job away from us, which would be our lives. But for as long as we have breath, we can go on in our wasteful ways. However, consider the act that is commendable to him: using possessions to gain favor, using "worldly wealth to gain friends for yourselves." Is he not straightforwardly telling us what to do with our wealth and resources? We have the ability to use our money, possessions, love, mercy, and grace to relieve others from their debt in ways they do not deserve, which in turn frees us from a punishment we do deserve. This theme of giving and forgiving shows up again and again in the New Testament. Consider James 2:13: "Judgment without mercy will be shown to anyone who has not been merciful. Mercy triumphs over judgment."

Have we not all been given the means by which to free ourselves? It costs us nothing because we ourselves own nothing, but we have been given the management power to hold for ourselves or freely give what we temporarily possess. Quickly, we should go about this business (Luke 16:6). The first order of business, however, is always to recognize the one who not only owns it all but who also owns us, having bought us with the price of his blood on a cross.

Money is powerful when it is not your master!
Its power is in giving it away. It holds no eternal
power or significance for those who possess it
solely for themselves, and it corrupts those who
love it. (1 Tim. 6:9–10, author's paraphrase)

42

Minimalism

In the spring of 2016, my company published an article on minimalism as the featured trend in our quarterly publication, *Lumen*. This was around the same time the documentary *Minimalism* came out. A few of my team members went to Grand Rapids for a screening of the film. It was an intriguing topic, and I found myself more and more drawn to the movement.

Minimalism can be defined in a variety of ways, but in essence it is voluntary simplicity. Choosing to get rid of stuff—our material possessions—can be freeing. It can open doors we didn't know existed, doors typically obstructed from view. Our stuff literally, and figuratively, gets in our way. Ironically, being surrounded by an abundance of stuff effectively limits us, not propels us as our culture would argue. Over time, we can't see the forest for the trees. Our assessment of our condition is obstructed by our belongings.

Simplification strategies have been around for decades, but what we are seeing today seems different, more radical. It will be interesting to watch it play out over time—will it be a passing fad or a wake-up call for our consumerist society? Some say the movement sprang out of the economic downturn and people being overwhelmed by insanely busy schedules. Whatever the motivation, this switch from consumerism to minimalism requires ongoing movement in the complete opposite direction. Consumerism encourages the acquisition of goods and services in ever-increasing amounts, creating a social and economic pecking order. Voluntary simplicity works in direct opposition to this hierarchy, creating an even more prominent contrast.

When I set out to understand more about minimalist living, I found plenty of resources: books, podcasts, Twitter feeds, and more (although, in the spirit of minimalism, I tried not to go overboard in what I consumed!). The deeper I got into understanding what this movement is all about—and again, I'm still just wading in the shallow waters here—the more benefits I began to see. And while the benefits of owning and consuming less are many, they also reach far beyond the realm of material goods. My dad used to repeat this quote often around the house: "The more stuff you have, the more stuff has you." While I have clearly overbought and at times allowed things to build up, I believe my accumulating ways have been somewhat lessened by hearing the voice of my father and living into the wisdom he passed on.

The other night, I was catching up at the office and ran out to get a bite to eat. As I was sitting at a table, friends of mine, Amy and Chris Kraal walked in. They stopped over to chat and shared that they had recently moved into a temporary apartment down the street from my office, a relatively small, two-bedroom place. They were beaming as they told me how this temporary move was having a profound effect on them. "We put our new-house building plans on ice," Amy said with excitement as she told me they were now considering living in their apartment for a number of years. "We got rid of a lot of stuff, and we are realizing how freeing it is to not have so much or owe so much." I was kind of stunned, I admit. I mean, their apartment was nice, but it wasn't even close to what they had been planning to do, not to mention how small it was in comparison.

Our friends Karyl and Mike Morin had a similar experience when they downsized and moved into a much smaller, simpler home. For them, the reduction of stuff was freeing, and they were surprised by the psychological benefits. Karyl shared with me recently that even though they got rid of at least half of their possessions, she was feeling like they still had too much—a true sign of a minimalist convert!

The biggest benefit of a simplified lifestyle is not so much what it frees you from but what it frees you to be.

To me the biggest benefit of a simplified lifestyle is not so much what it *frees* you from but what it frees you to *be*. It is an unshackling of sorts, particularly on your time and attention. Let me set the record straight: I am not a minimalist (yet). I like to say, however, I'm a recovering materialist. There are merits to this movement and power in its core principles, many of which were perfectly displayed in how Jesus lived on earth.

Jesus was perhaps one of the greatest minimalists of all time. Not only did he live in an extremely simple way, but he called others into that way of life as well. "Go, sell your possessions and give to the poor" or some variation on this statement was recurring counsel Jesus gave to individuals, as well as a theme found in many of his parables.

Reduction seems to have a happiness component to it. This is what Amy and Chris and Karyl and Mike found in their downsizing. Reducing brings relief, which pairs with the joy of giving; you end up with a double hit of happiness. There is clearly a link between generosity and joy. My family lives in Holland, Michigan, which was recently ranked one of the happiest towns in the United States (in spite of the constant cloud cover and harsh winters). I don't think it's a coincidence that Holland is also one of the most philanthropic communities in the country.

Truth be told, I often perceive the commands within Scripture to be burdensome and heavy, and yet Jesus says, "Come to me, all you who are weary and burdened, and I will give you rest. Take my yoke upon you and learn from me, for I am gentle and humble in heart, and you will find rest for your souls. For my yoke is easy and my burden is light" (Matt. 11:28–30). When I hear these words, I think of those who have been releasing not just their stuff but also their burdens and their fears. Jesus calls us over and over again into a soulful rest. I'm realizing afresh how wise it is to spend time with Jesus, to invest time in his Word in order to observe how he lived, to study what he said, and to integrate all of this into my life through the power of his Spirit. God's Word is always counsel for our ultimate good, a safe harbor in life's storms.

> "Do not store up for yourselves treasures on earth, where moths and vermin destroy, and where thieves break in and steal. But store up for yourselves treasures in heaven, where moths and vermin do not destroy, and where thieves do not break in and steal. For where your treasure is, there your heart will be also." (Matt. 6:19–21)

43

Misaligned Value

"What people value highly is detestable in God's sight" (Luke 16:15). Jesus directed this damning statement toward a group of Pharisees he was addressing. These Pharisees, Jewish religious leaders of Jesus's day, had lost their way. They had drifted so far from God they failed to recognize Jesus in the flesh. They worshiped man-made rules as a means of justification and honor before men. This, along with their growing power and position within the temple and the nation (John 11:48), caused them to slip into the grip of greed and wickedness. All of this was covered under the veneer of righteous behavior. All the while, they ignored their true inner selves. This is akin to a beautiful home full of termites, where the perceived value of the home does not reflect its actual value.

It is not hard to figure out what people value highly, is it? People prize being esteemed and counted as important by other people. Meanwhile, God is looking for people who highly value him above all.

What I find amazing about Jesus is his unashamed, overt, in-your-face, verbal undressing that exposes reality. This is something he alone could do, for only he knew the hidden intentions and motives of those around him. This is what made him so polarizing then, and it is what makes him so polarizing now. Not because he could cut through the crap (which he often did without reservation). And not because he was inconsiderate or rude or insensitive. No, he did this because it was the only way to awaken them (and us) to the reality of their condition.

In truth, we all have two sides to ourselves: the side we show the world and the side we try to keep hidden. This is not to say we never expose who we are to others, but it's rare that we do. Imagine hanging out with Jesus, knowing he could expose you any time you acted in a way that was counter to your stated values or any time you chose inaction rather than acting on your values. How unsettling and uncomfortable would that be! It wouldn't take long before you'd see your lack of transparency about who you really are or before you see the fact you care more about impressing those around you than living for God. This would hurt and awaken you at the same time. Thankfully, Jesus is not calling us out in front of others. This is why, however, it is so imperative we read his words in Scripture, since that is where he does convict us—but only *if* we are honest and willing to see ourselves in the text. As my father-in-law often likes to remind people, we play to an audience of one.

We are not alone in our struggle to align our actions and our values. Even the great apostle Paul agonized over the two sides of who he was.

> So I find this law at work: Although I want to do good, evil is right there with me. For in my inner being I delight in God's law; but I see another law at work in me, waging war against the law of my mind and

making me a prisoner of the law of sin at work within me. What a wretched man I am! Who will rescue me from this body that is subject to death? Thanks be to God, who delivers me through Jesus Christ our Lord!

So then, I myself in my mind am a slave to God's law, but in my sinful nature a slave to the law of sin. (Rom. 7:21–25)

Paul had Christ resident within him and knew that God through Jesus was the answer to his predicament, a predicament we all face each and every day. For every day we are in need of rescue from our old self, our sin nature. We know our true self is found only in God, who resides in us. God is seeking to restore us to our true identity by dwelling with and within us. Surrendering to his residence is the answer.

He wants nothing more than to deliver us from ourselves and our misaligned values. But we so easily forget, don't we? We need to be reminded over and over that what humans value highly is detestable to God. I should write this out and put up signs around my home and business to remind myself and keep it at the forefront of my mind rather than settling for the faint recollection it so often becomes. God will not compete with the airtime of what humans value highly. The voice of God is heard when we seek it, and often it is little more than a gentle whisper (1 Kings 19:12). Conversely, the clashing voices of man-made, cultural values engulf us, screaming for our attention throughout our day. We are bombarded with these ideals. We are told what we should do, what we should buy, and what we should be in order to obtain high value in the world's eyes. It is a never-ending trap. Just when I think I've managed to escape it, I find myself back in its grip, again and again.

What is even worse than being constantly fooled by these false values is beginning to believe this fleeting life is all there is, that each day will be the same as the day before. Only when I step back and reflect can I get a glimpse of the eternal. As difficult as it is for me to grasp an eternal perspective, I must do it; it is the remedy to a wasted life. I long to live in light of eternity, for only in this space can I recognize the flaws in what humans value highly, what I value highly. In the light of the eternal, I can see my physical life as brief and, oh, so temporary against the backdrop of the infinite. Why would I want to waste a single day highly valuing detestable things? I need to live awakened to the reality that all earthly things are temporary. Yes, whatever people value highly is detestable to God.

In the light of the eternal, I can see my physical life as brief and, oh, so temporary against the backdrop of the infinite.

My mother- and father-in-law, Mary and Jim, will often say, "Only God, his Word, and people will last. Invest yourself there." What a great reminder of the things I need to re-center and recalibrate my values around: God, his Word, and people. Investing anywhere else, highly valuing anything else, is utter foolishness.

FAITH IN
ACTION

44

Reviving Love

The few years leading up to my mother's passing were marked with a growing discontent. I was yearning for more—more of what mattered and more of God's heart to be evident in me. From sleepless nights to countless conversations with friends, God was stirring within me a holy dissatisfaction with my life.

Shortly after Mom passed, I was filled with a sense of urgency unlike any I had felt before. I pushed myself to understand how I could be more laser-focused in my second half of life. What did God have in store for me to do in this season?

This led me to a unique training opportunity in Atlanta in early January of 2018. It was an intensive four-day program appropriately named "Younique" that was designed to help individuals uncover their life's calling through an assessment of their natural strengths, spiritual gifts, and life experiences. The workshop included many hours of introspection and prayer. At the end, participants presented their clearly articulated calling to the group. We all started narrowly, only permitted to use two words. Mine were *reviving love*. Reviving love was primarily about revitalizing my personal love for God and discovering the deeper layers of God's love for me and my response to it. "We love because he first loved us" (1 John 4:19). Although I have expanded reviving love to a broader scope, the core is still centered on Matthew 22:37–39: "'Love the Lord your God with all your heart and with all your soul and with all your mind.' This is the first and greatest commandment. And the second is like it: 'Love your neighbor as yourself.'" Yes, love for God is the first and greatest commandment. I have been seeking to understand how this plays out practically, naturally, and supernaturally in my own life and, somehow, the life of my neighbor as well. I have newly discovered how intrinsically linked these two commandments are to each other. Living into the meaning of one entails living into the other. Jesus couldn't have made it clearer when he said, "And the second is like it: 'Love your neighbor as yourself'" (Matt. 22:39).

Reviving love, for me, is also about communicating what I'm learning, which can take many forms, one of which is this book. Whatever the shape or mode, it must spring from a sincere, honest, and authentic heart. It must focus on God and neighbor and on authentically living into a love for both. In short, I discovered God calling me to be a more intentional doer of the greatest commandment and encourager of others to do the same.

Of course, living into the first commandment is a call for all believers, but just because all are instructed to do so does not mean everyone is embracing or understanding it to the degree Jesus intended. I certainly was not. This golden rule is age-old— as familiar as many nursery rhymes or Sunday school songs— yet after this workshop, God awakened me to the significant impact it could have on myself and others if expressed and lived out purely and humbly. But as with so many truths, communicating it was the easy part; living it out would be much harder.

Jesus embodied this twofold command through focusing on the disenfranchised neighbor. This is not surprising given he was arguably the most disenfranchised of all—born poor, an immigrant on the run, homeless throughout his ministry, rejected by his own, beaten to within an inch of his life, and brutally crucified on a cross.

I now see my neighbor as anyone who is marginalized, oppressed, or in greater need than myself. And it doesn't leave out someone I may disdain. This was the neighbor Jesus described through the story of the good Samaritan, when asked by an expert in the law, "Who is my neighbor?" (See Luke 10:29–37). It's impossible not to tie love for God to love for neighbor. They are intrinsically linked. Jesus clearly states the second command is like the first.

This past year I have been more aware of the needs of those around me and have become more active in meeting needs as I have deepened my understanding of how I tangibly express my love for God. Teaching in a prison, sharing resources in unconventional ways, and intentionally allowing time to sit with suffering souls to just listen or gently encourage has rekindled a love for both God and others that simply was not there before. I am discovering that acts of generosity can magnify love in both the giver and the receiver.

The love and care for neighbor is the most sacred of acts because we are not only the hands and feet of Jesus; we are expressing our love for God.

How exactly this works is a mystery of sorts, one that continues to unfold each time I choose to love in concrete ways. How is it I've overlooked this spiritual truth that is clearly stated in God's Word? I want generous love to become my reality, my spiritual practice of experiencing and reviving love. The love and care for neighbor is the most sacred of acts because we are not only the hands and feet of Jesus; we are expressing our love for God.

Our responsibility for and kindness towards our neighbor is so powerful that Jesus cites it as evidence of true, believing faith prior to welcoming his followers into heaven (Matt. 25:31–46). Do I need more motivation than that?

45

God, Neighbor, and You

"I must stay at your house today." Jesus took an improbable turn to walk up to the base of a sycamore tree, looking up to find this one man. We don't know what was behind his insistence on staying with Zacchaeus, but we do know that this man was surprised to be found. "Zacchaeus, come down immediately. I must stay at your house today." Jesus found him and even knew him by name. This event, recorded in Luke 19:1–10, depicts Jesus passing through the town of Jericho amidst the crowds gathered to see him. Imagine how honoring it felt that Jesus, whom the large crowds were clamoring to see, wanted to stay at his house. Zacchaeus "welcomed him gladly" (v. 6). Immediately, a negative crowd reaction ensued. The crowd was as shocked as Zacchaeus, and perhaps for the same reason: Jesus "has gone to be the guest of a sinner" (v. 7).

Did Zacchaeus even notice the crowd muttering? This small man stood tall and made a pronouncement directly to his Lord, "Look, Lord! Here and now I give half of my possessions to the poor, and if I have cheated anybody out of anything, I will pay back four times the amount" (v. 8). Jesus's response may have also had the crowds muttering. "Today salvation has come to this house, because this man, too, is a son of Abraham. For the Son of Man came to seek and to save the lost." Zacchaeus's heart was changed suddenly through this encounter with Jesus, the Lord of all. The change was as immediate as the shock of being singled out.

Why did Jesus announce Zacchaeus's salvation after Zacchaeus announced his intent to give generously to the poor and all those he had wronged? Does it seem odd that Jesus proclaims Zacchaeus's salvation without Zacchaeus making any specific proclamation of allegiance to Jesus? Yes, he addresses him as Lord, but as Jesus states in Matthew 7:21, "Not everyone who says to me, 'Lord, Lord,' will enter the kingdom of heaven, but only the one who does the will of my Father who is in heaven." The sequence of events in this story—let alone the extraordinary generosity—may seem foreign to present-day followers of Jesus. Doesn't a saving knowledge and acceptance of Jesus as Lord begin with a prayer? Traditionally, it takes time to learn to give a portion back to God through tithing. How eye-opening that Jesus gave no cautions, no suggested adjustments, and no corrections of any kind! It was as if there was no difference between Zacchaeus's newfound love for God and his actions of love for his neighbor. Zacchaeus's rebirth manifested itself in an immediate reaction of giving to others. A similar active response is duplicated by new believers in Acts 2:45. They sold their property and possessions and gave to anyone who had need. Clearly, Jesus is honored and displayed as Lord through believers' actions of generosity toward those in need. No clarification was offered; no clarification was required. Simply put, generosity to those in need is an expression of Jesus being one's Lord, the manifestation of a heart change.

Zacchaeus's demonstration of his love for God was through his love for his neighbor. Our love for God and love for our neighbor are synonymous, a mirror for each other, demonstrating genuine change. And Jesus received Zacchaeus's demonstration of his love for him through his sacrificial gift to the poor. It was obvious to all who knew Zacchaeus that he was not capable of this type of generosity on his own. Jesus was the force behind the act. Zacchaeus was not the same man; this was a radical change in who he was at his core. It was none other than God transforming a sinful man into a God-natured man—a man that gives, seeks, and loves the broken, downcast, and poor.

Our love for God and love for our neighbor are synonymous, a mirror for each other, demonstrating genuine change.

Our love for God finds its expression in our love for our neighbor. These actions allow an unseen God to be revealed—a miracle that generously blesses both. This is such a fitting response of our transformed heart, or perhaps it is the first step of active faith, preceding the full change of heart.

> For the entire law is fulfilled in keeping
> this one command: "Love your neighbor
> as yourself." (Galatians 5:14)

46

Best Decision Ever

When Chris first came to me to talk about the possibility of adopting, I wasn't exactly receptive. It wasn't that I was against the idea of adoption; it had more to do with my "that ship has sailed" mentality. After all, I was nearly forty, and we had four boys under our roof, ranging from preschool to seventh grade. Since we had only planned on having two or three children when we first started out, five was just a bit much for me to get my head around. Although, if we were going to have a girl, adoption was certainly a safe gender bet.

My best friend, Mark, gave a toast at our wedding. He had encouraged us to have many children. He even recited Psalm 127:4–5: "Like arrows in the hands of a warrior are children born in one's youth. Blessed is the man whose quiver is full of them." At the time, I found his words really funny. The eventual realization of his prophetic words was, well, sobering.

It didn't take me long to warm up to adoption. Honestly, I feared if God had placed the desire on Chris's heart for us to adopt (which it seemed he had), who was I to stand in the way? I was also concerned with facing God at the end of my life having said no to his will and shunning his prompts. I had done enough of that in my life already. When we began in earnest to work through the process, it became exciting.

Early on, Chris desired confirmation and prayed for a sign from God prior to us sending in the initial application. She received it a few days later. Sitting alone at the kitchen table, opening the mail, she came upon a Christmas card from Mrs. Moore, a dear friend who was a bit of a mother figure to Chris. As she opened the card, a picture fell out and landed face up. It was a picture of a young Chinese girl—Mrs. Moore's new adopted granddaughter. Chris knew immediately in her heart this was God's confirming touch. As Chris looked down at this picture, she sensed God looking down on her, smiling and affirming the desire of her heart, a desire that aligned with his.

> *God, in his grace, gave this joy and this restoration through her to us and through us to her.*

While the unknowns were scary at times, the journey was worth it. It was a challenging process as the SARS (Severe Acute Respiratory Syndrome) epidemic in China prolonged it by an additional four months. During this time, I also lost my job, and our commitment was tested. But isn't that always the way it is? Faith is not faith without obstacles to test it and hardships to prove it (James 1:3).

I asked if I could name our daughter, and Chris agreed. There was no name search, no asking people to weigh in on a myriad of options, no debate. As clear as God had given Chris the desire to adopt, he had given me her name—Grace. For God, in his grace, allowed us to adopt this amazing child. God, in his grace, supplied her with a family that adores her. God, in his grace, gave this joy and this restoration through her to us and through us to her.

The day our Wisconsin home sold, after being on the market

for six months, was also the day we received the notification that Grace had been matched with us, and we received a photo. Lying on our bed, her picture in hand, we felt similarly to when each of our newborn sons had nestled between us. When we finally held her in our arms in Guangzhou, China, she completely melted our hearts. The most amazing aspect of adoption for us was the miracle of assimilation. Grace became our child, and there was no difference between her and our boys. She became a Bakker. In every aspect of our lives, we became one. She became our daughter, and we became her parents. I can't articulate the depth of this or even how it occurs. I can only testify that it happens on a spiritual, emotional, and relational level.

Our adoption journey has also given us a much greater appreciation of what it means to be adopted into God's family, through Christ. All who are in Christ have been adopted into the family of God, a reality that is made possible through Christ's finished work on the cross. It's so easy to gloss over this truth, but we need to linger over it and let it sink in. We have become sons and daughters of God! We are heirs and coheirs with Christ. We are no longer alone, without hope or a future home; instead, we are the King's children, precious and loved. We are his, bought with the greatest sacrifice anyone could give: his very life.

> For those who are led by the Spirit of God are the children of God. The Spirit you received does not make you slaves, so that you live in fear again; rather, the Spirit you received brought about your adoption to sonship. And by him we cry, "*Abba*, Father." The Spirit himself testifies with our spirit that we are God's children. Now if we are children, then we are heirs—heirs of God and co-heirs with Christ, if indeed we share in his sufferings in order that we may also share in his glory. (Rom. 8:14–17)

Looking back, we see this was one of the best decisions we have ever made on so many levels. I'm so grateful for Chris's prayerful and faithful following of God's direction for us. Grace has brought each member of our family joy beyond measure.

47

Actions Speak

He posed the request to both of his sons. There was so much work that needed to be attended to, and he desperately needed their help.

He spoke first to his oldest son, Dan. Irritated by the request for a hand, Dan blurted out, "No, I won't!" His father was taken aback by the immediacy of his reply. But as disappointed as he was with his son's response, he didn't have time to argue or persuade. Instead, he focused on locating his other son, Jeff.

"Yes, father," Jeff replied. "Of course, I'll help. Right away." The father was relieved by his younger son's immediate willingness to go to work. Such a good kid! At the same time, however, he was disheartened by his other son's response. After all he had done for him, could Dan not formulate a more respectful response than "No, I won't"?

Later that day the man stopped in to check on Jeff and see how things were going. To his surprise, Jeff was nowhere to be found. Instead, Dan was hard at work, sweat pouring down his face.

"Dan, what are you doing here? You said no when I asked you to help."

Dan smiled in a conflicted sort of way. "Yeah Dad, I changed my mind. I shouldn't have responded the way I did. After all you've done for me, the least I could do is help you out." He turned back to the task at hand, committed to seeing it to completion.

> "What do you think? There was a man who had two sons. He went to the first and said, 'Son, go and work today in the vineyard.'
>
> "'I will not,' he answered, but later he changed his mind and went.
>
> "Then the father went to the other son and said the same thing. He answered, 'I will, sir,' but he did not go.
>
> "Which of the two did what his father wanted?"
>
> "The first," they answered. (Matt. 21:28–31)

This parable has always been intriguing to me. If ever there was a lesson of action over words, this is it. It is interesting how the focus is on the work, which is synonymous with the will of the father. The responses are telling but secondary. The no response was wiped out by the yes action. Conversely, the yes response was wiped out by the no action.

It is so easy to say yes; the follow-through is the hard part. Conversely, it is hard to say no and harder still to change one's mind toward action. The first son gave an honest reaction—"I will not"—but then changed his mind. We don't know if the second son had no intention of going or if he had a change of heart after some reflection. Or perhaps something else came up that took him away from his promise? This would be analogous to the seeds that fell among thorns in Matthew's parable of the sower.

"Other seed fell among thorns, which grew up and choked the plants" (Matt. 13:7).

These are disruptive parables. Let's face it: following God is so much more than a simple yes—even an eager, well-intentioned yes. Engagement is the evidence of commitment, and ongoing engagement is the evidence of true, ongoing faith, a faith that will not falter when distractions come along, when hardships hit, when temptations pull, when, when, when.

The initial yes—whether kneeling publicly at the altar or saying a quiet prayer at home—is not a complete yes. Neither is an initial no final. If a no can turn into a yes and a yes can turn into a no by means of engagement or lack of engagement in the work, then could one conclude that the initial response is irrelevant? Actions are the words of the kingdom.

That seems so strange to say the response of a yes or a no is irrelevant to our relationship with God. Clearly, today we are in search of the yes. A simple hand raised at the end of a message indicating a decision for Christ is what some are hanging their hats on, is it not? Don't get me wrong, I'm all about people making decisions for Christ in a public way. But it cannot stop there. The yes must be an active and ongoing agreement, otherwise it is actually a no. It is really that simple and that life altering. There is just no getting around it.

> *Engagement is the evidence of commitment, and ongoing engagement is the evidence of true, ongoing faith.*

Consider these words of Jesus in John's Gospel, where he draws a connection between obedience to his commands and love for God.

"If you love me, keep my commands." (John 14:15)

"Whoever has my commands and keeps them is the one who loves me. The one who loves me will

221

be loved by my Father, and I too will love them and show myself to them." (John 14:21)

Jesus replied, "Anyone who loves me will obey my teaching. My Father will love them, and we will come to them and make our home with them." (John 14:23)

"Anyone who does not love me will not obey my teaching. These words you hear are not my own; they belong to the Father who sent me." (John 14:24)

"As the Father has loved me, so have I loved you. Now remain in my love. If you keep my commands, you will remain in my love, just as I have kept my Father's commands and remain in his love." (John 15:9–10)

Actions do not speak louder than words. Actions *are* the words of the kingdom.

It's clear that the will of the Father is for us to engage in kingdom work. Listen to how Jesus ends this dialogue with the religious leaders with whom he had just shared the parable of the two sons: "'Truly I tell you, the tax collectors and the prostitutes are entering the kingdom of God ahead of you. For John came to you to show you the way of righteousness, and you did not believe him, but the tax collectors and the prostitutes did. And even after you saw this, you did not repent and believe him'" (Matt. 21:31–32).

Jesus makes it clear that sinful tax collectors and prostitutes heard and responded to the message of the gospel—responded, repented, and engaged in kingdom work. Meanwhile, the religious, even after witnessing this miracle of change in the most sinful of lives, refused to repent or believe the message John was preaching. Jesus shows us that any life, regardless of its sinful state, can be redeemed through the actions of repentance and pursuing the kingdom work of righteous obedience. He also shows us that a polished life void of true obedience, as was true for many of the religious leaders, is a worthless life with no need to repent, no need to change, no need to engage in messy kingdom work. Many then, and now, say yes with their words but demonstrate through their inaction that their answer, in the end, is no.

> *Lord, how many times have I lived a no in my relationship with you? How many times have I appeared to be living a yes through my words but failed to act on your clear teaching? Help me to remember I am your handiwork, to recognize the good work you have prepared for me to do, and to faithfully remain engaged in it. Amen.*

48

Closing the Gap

There is such disparity in our world today, an ever-widening gap between the rich and the poor. Before I traveled overseas on my first visit to a developing country, I knew only intellectually about the plight of the abject poor through what I had heard, read, or seen on TV. I was not prepared for confronting the reality firsthand. It was gut-wrenching.

My first trip was sparked by reading the book *Radical* by David Platt. A friend of mine, Steve Ridgeway, recommended it to me saying, "This book will change your life. You will never be the same, and I am sorry in advance." Of course, I ran out and got the book and read it cover to cover. Steve was right; it did alter my life, and ripples of the message still affect me. In the book, Platt lays out the radical call to action, as outlined in Scripture, against the backdrop of the American Dream. It is a challenging book to read, but it is far more challenging to implement. The call to action I immediately committed to was to live two percent of that year in a developing nation, rather than in my typical context. I saw it as the most demanding, risky, and shocking suggestion from Platt. I was longing for a radical change, not just a minor adjustment to my lifestyle, so I reasoned that doing this would surely have that effect.

A sense of urgency after reading this book so filled me that I called my trusted friend Mark to see if we could meet. Mark leads a campus ministry and has traveled overseas many times. He had one open slot that day, which normally wouldn't be a problem, except Mark lives an hour and a half away.

"Mark, this is extremely important," I said. "I have to see you today."

As long as I was willing to drive his way, he was willing to meet that very day. We sat down at a McDonalds in Cedar Springs, Michigan, for the quickest meeting ever—ten minutes—but that was all I needed. Mark was sitting in the booth sipping on a Coke with a smile on his face when I sat down across from him, not even bothering to order food or drink—no time for that. He listened intently as I shared how what I had read impacted me, and I had to go overseas soon. I wanted him to join me. He saw the urgency in my eyes and agreed to go.

"Mark, you won't regret this," I said. "And by the way, could you plan it? You've been overseas, and I have no clue what I'm doing. I don't care where, so long as it's in a place where we can help the marginalized."

With that, Mark left, and I hopped back in the car for my hour-long drive home.

Mark discovered an organization in Haiti called Love a Child and planned a trip during spring break. I thought back to an earlier conversation I had with Josh, our second son, who was now in his second year of college. Before Josh left for college, he had been questioning his faith—not in a bad way, but the sort of healthy questioning that parents pray will lead to their children to owning their faith rather than simply believing what their parents told them to believe. So I asked Josh if he would be interested in going with us, fully anticipating a rejection. He answered, however, without so much as a pause: "Yes!" I reiterated to him that this was over his spring break. He was on the football team at an academically challenging college; Haiti was not going to be restful. Josh understood and assured me that yes was his final answer.

I hardly knew what to expect on this trip. I was nervous and excited. When I checked in with Josh before the trip, he remained resolute, which both surprised and delighted me.

The trip was more than either of us had hoped. During the day, we worked on a large housing project, and at night, we had time to visit and tour the compound. One night we joined a worship service in the orphanage. The kids sang songs in words we didn't understand, and many of the smaller ones would sit nearby or on the laps of the volunteers. It was at that service Josh encountered the Spirit of God more powerfully than he ever had. The experience that night and the long talks he had with Mark changed him. The trip shifted the trajectory of Josh's life, as this is where he came face-to-face with the Spirit of God and gave his heart to Jesus.

That first trip, in the spring of 2011, kick-started a process of change not only for Josh but for me as well—a change in our perspectives of the world, a change in our purposes. Yes, it felt good to help those who were hurting and less fortunate, but at the same time it left me feeling helpless, with a growing sense that I could do more, that I *should* do more. Each trip after that increasingly opened my eyes to the excess we have compared with much of the rest of the world.

In July 2012, on a return flight from Zambia, Africa, I was feeling especially helpless against the poverty and need I had witnessed. I had seen firsthand how Poetice International compassionately worked to restore the psychological, relational, spiritual, emotional, and physical realities that are distorted in the lives of people experiencing poverty. Much of this centered on the holistic development of orphans and vulnerable children, first by identifying specific children and then by coming alongside them. One facet of this transformational effort entailed making education, health care, and food economically accessible. On our trip, we enjoyed building relationships with the children through visiting their homes, which were often little more than a tent, through taking the time to sit and talk, and through bringing them gifts.

Seth, our middle son, accompanied me on this first trip to Zambia at the young age of seventeen. I dare say even though the conditions in certain areas were not good, we had a remarkable experience, particularly at the camp where kids gathered from many neighborhoods to worship and learn. It took Seth a few days to warm up, but after that, the smile on his face never dimmed. Those Zambian boys surrounded him with laughter, warmth, and love.

The conditions of poverty were heartbreaking, but more heartbreaking were the vast numbers of children who couldn't be helped because the resources weren't available. I felt like we were climbing over those in desperate need to help those who were slightly worse off. I could go on and on about the catastrophic devastation brought on by HIV/AIDS and how most of the children are orphans or double orphans because their parents died from the epidemic. Likewise, I could go on and on about the powerful change happening through Poetice and the restorative work that is coming about through the generosity of people led by God's Spirit. And still, even knowing about this good work, I struggle immensely with the scale of the need.

It continues to be difficult for me to reconcile the disparities in the world today. Pain, hurt, starvation, and disease are spread all over the world. But that doesn't lessen the need for each of us to go and to give. One bright spot for me, a source of hope in the midst of the world's pain, is all four of our boys—Josh, David, Seth, and Luke—have heeded this call to go and to give. It has been a privilege to help make it possible for them to travel overseas on multiple mission trips, to Haiti, Zambia, Guatemala, and Jamaica. Each of them has been impacted by God's working, and I trust that their hearts will continue to expand as they go to the places God calls them.

I love the story of a man who, while walking along the beach, sees someone in the distance throwing starfish into the ocean. The tide had been unusually high, and thousands upon thousands of starfish had gotten caught beyond the water's reach; they would almost certainly die unless someone threw them back in. When he finally got close enough to the man throwing the starfish back, he asked, "What are you doing? You can't possibly think you're going to make a difference with the thousands of starfish on this beach!" The other man bent down, grabbed another starfish, and threw it into the ocean. "I did for that one!"

This is certainly how I have felt many times. I cannot possibly make a difference for everyone in need. No one person can. But doing nothing disregards those for whom we can make a difference and ignores the work that God has prepared for us to do. "For we are God's handiwork, created in Christ Jesus to do good works, which God prepared in advance for us to do" (Eph. 2:10).

> But doing nothing disregards those for whom we can make a difference and ignores the work that God has prepared for us to do.

This is what is so amazing, not just about each one of us but about the collective body of Christ. The church has been his design from day one, and the church is a strong collective body that can, does, and will continue to make a difference here and throughout the world. I love God's plan for the collective group, the church, and I'm humbled by my individual call—a call to love all my neighbors, including the one next door, the one in the grade school down the street, the ones in the prison up north, and the ones who are hurting across the ocean.

Lord, continue to show me what you would have me do specifically, the very work you have prepared for me. Amen.

49

Parallel Worlds

On the morning of September 3, 2012, I woke up in my hotel room with a story floating around in my head, so I grabbed my tablet and began to type. What I wrote was a vision of sorts, something I'm sure was informed by my first trip to Haiti the previous year, where I encountered poverty and despair up close for the first time. I had struggled greatly to reconcile my life in the States with what I had witnessed there, and this reflection was part of that process for me.

Imagine you won an all-expense-paid vacation to the Cayman Islands. You arrive, check in, and begin to stroll around your room. It's beyond glorious. Just beyond your balcony is an amazing panoramic view of the ocean with the pool below you. It's stunning, absolutely stunning!

To your surprise, on your very first night there, you hear the faint, almost-whispering voices of children crying—far away cries, off in the distance. You call down to the front desk and inquire. The woman listens and offers an apology. She goes on to tell you that you are one of the rare few that have visited their resort who has experienced this phenomenon. "Somehow you have been allowed to experience and see things that evade most," she explains.

You don't understand what you've just been told, but you're determined to have a great time, even if it means blocking out this annoying distraction. After all, if others are having a great time here, why can't you?

The next day the sun is shining, so you head down to the beach. You lay out your towel and start reading your book. Again, you hear the cries, but this time they are slightly louder. You look up from your book, and to your surprise, you are surrounded not by the fit, bronzed bodies of the privileged who were there moments ago but by starving, sickly, diseased-looking children and adults. The kids are trying to drink from a hole filled with dirty, germ-infested water.

You get up from your towel and go down to the ocean's edge. Bodies float face down in the water. A knowing begins to creep over you, a thought you can't shake: each one could have been spared, but there was no one there to help them, to save them.

Slowly, what you see around you at the beach returns to normal, and the vision fades back to the way things were.

But your perspective has shifted dramatically since you first heard the faint cries in the distance. You try to hide it, but you are visibly shaken. How is it possible you are the only one experiencing this? Out of compulsion, you begin to query other people who are staying at the resort: "Excuse me, but do you at times see suffering people all around us?" All of them are quick to say no, accompanied by a look that says, "What's wrong with you?" They all see stunning views, a gorgeous resort, and delicious food, nothing more.

Clearly, the other resort guests have now categorized you as certifiably crazy, and somehow this doesn't bother you nearly as much as it should. You begin to view these people through a different lens. They seem shallow and superficial, more concerned about where and what they are going to eat than about who isn't going to eat that day. More worried about whether they remembered to set out a towel to save the special spot by the pool. More interested in whether the bartender will be that cute college intern that was there yesterday. Shallow and superficial, yes—just like you a few days ago.

That night at dinner, you sit down, hungry but perplexed by what is happening. Bracing yourself for what's coming next, you order. (So far so good. Nothing out of the ordinary.) The waiter brings out your meal, and you begin cutting your steak. But as you're bringing the first bite up to your mouth, you notice an emaciated child with an empty plate just a few tables away. Moved by compassion, you walk over to offer him some of your steak. But as you get closer, he slowly morphs into a large, overweight man surrounded by enough food to feed a small village.

"Can I help you?" he asks with juice running down his chin onto the bib wrapped around his thick neck.

Standing in front of him, semi-embarrassed, holding a piece of steak with your fork, all you can manage to say is, "No, I'm sorry. I didn't mean to interrupt you."

As you're walking back to your table, you overhear his wife say, "He's the crazy one I told you about. The one who sees things."

It occurs to you that your visions are more than just figments of your imagination. Sure, it's possible you're crazy, but deep down you know you're in your right mind. And even though you can't fully understand what's happening, it feels like you're awakening to what is real, despite what the majority says, a majority you now view as asleep. The suffering ones you have experienced, whose eyes you have looked into, they are real to you. But you can't reach them from where you are. You have to go to them, and you cannot go to them unless you're willing to take risks—costly risks, perhaps costing you everything you have. You know you're being called to go, so the remaining question is, Are you willing? And really, what choice do you have?

And even though you can't fully understand what's happening, it feels like you're awakening to what is real, despite what the majority says, a majority you now view as asleep.

You run up to the woman at the front desk, the same one you chatted with your first night here. "Excuse me, but you told me about the few who have experienced what I am experiencing. Can you tell me what became of them?"

"Sure," she replies. "Many of them still vacation with us, but over time their visions have faded, and they no longer hear or see anything. Honestly, they don't seem happy. They seem like they are going through the motions. It sounds strange to say, but they act as if they are guilty of a crime. They look to each other to be reassured all is well, like being freed by a jury of your peers or something. They seem numb and more distant with each visit."

Her look penetrates your being. "There are a few who have followed the vision while it is still clear to them. They pay a big price; some of them have died in the process. They travel far to assist where they can, feed the hungry, clothe and love the less fortunate. I enjoy hearing their stories on the rare occasion they find their way back here. They are full of joy and heartache at the same time. It's hard to tell if their hearts are broken more for the starving children or for the soul-starved guests at this resort. They spend their time here searching out guests who can see and hear the visions and pleading with them to come along on their next trip. These trips could cost all they have (Matt. 13:44), but they claim they come with rewards unlike any they have ever experienced, with security and treasure on the other side."

"The seed falling among the thorns refers to
someone who hears the word, but the worries of
this life and the deceitfulness of wealth choke
the word, making it unfruitful." (Matt. 13:22)

If one of you says to them, "Go in peace;
keep warm and well fed," but does nothing
about their physical needs, what good is it?
In the same way, faith by itself, if it is not
accompanied by action, is dead. (James 2:16–17)

50

The Greatest

A sincere voice called out from the wilderness, "Repent, for the kingdom of heaven has come near," (Matt. 3:2). Imagine how strange this must have been: an unkempt man wearing clothes made from camel's hair, boldly making unfamiliar proclamations and appealing to anyone within earshot to repent. Stranger still, a growing contingency of people did not dismiss him as mad or crazy. Rather, they were drawn to him, confessing their sins and being baptized by him in the Jordan River. His name was John, known to us as John the Baptist. A simple man with a simple, unwavering message. His ministry was a short six months, but his story and his message live on each time the gospel is preached. John's mission and message could have been anticipated, as his journey was foretold years before by the Old Testament prophet Isaiah. Yet, like Jesus, his arrival took people by surprise, and he was a threat to the ruling religious party.

John was ordained by God, and miracles marked his life. Even before he was born, God's hand was on John. John leapt in his mother's womb when Mary, pregnant with Jesus, walked into the room (Luke 1:41). The same Spirit that caused John to leap in the womb led his steps and gave him his message, a message of preparation for his Lord's ministry (Luke 7:27). The Holy Spirit drew people to his bold proclamations of repentance.

John was no ordinary man. In fact, Jesus made a declaration about John that is downright unbelievable: "I tell you, among those born of women there is no one greater than John" (Luke 7:28). No one greater? No one outside of Jesus himself! Jesus considered John the greatest, greater than other renowned leaders like David, Moses, Isaiah, and Abraham. What had John done that would cause the Creator of all to adorn him with the most honorable title ever given to a man? Jesus made this stunning proclamation not merely because it was true but more so to cause us to take note of the life and message of John.

John was chosen and set apart at conception to prepare the way for God in the flesh. He was filled with the Holy Spirit. John's mission was clear and given directly from God. Even his name was ordained by God (Luke 1:13). John didn't need much in the way of comforts. He lived off of locusts and honey and had a singular focus: to commune with God and to fulfill his calling. His life was not his own; it was given over for God's kingdom purposes.

John was set apart and lived a life devoted to God. No scandals to report, no affairs, no murders, no half-truths. John was not perfect, but he was sold-out to his calling. He was not sinless, but he was repentant. John didn't consider himself worthy, but he leaned into his identity in God. He who was the greatest was also humble. His greatness lay in his devotion to his calling.

John was all about promoting Jesus, not drawing attention to himself. When the attention pivoted away from him to Jesus, he rejoiced. When people wondered if John might possibly be the Messiah, John answered them, "I baptize you with water. But one who is more powerful than I will come, the straps of whose sandals I am not worthy to untie. He will baptize you with the Holy Spirit and fire" (Luke 3:16).

The greatest was always on mission, pointing to Jesus and preparing the hearts of his hearers to take action to receive Jesus. He was a human billboard announcing the coming of the Son of God. The cover charge to receive him: turn back toward God. First and foremost, repent! "Repent, for the kingdom of heaven has come near" (Matt. 3:2).

John's message was not a lengthy dissertation. It was simple and right to the point. And yet, a radical, life-altering heart transformation was necessary to obey his message. His message was a call to change direction—the 180-degree variety. Repentance is a change of heart and mind that results in a change of action. Jesus himself affirmed this message when he began preaching, his first recorded words from his first message were identical to John's: "Repent, for the kingdom of heaven has come near" (Matt. 4:17).

What is our response to John's message today? Is he not calling us in the same way? The timeless truth of John's message has not faded, but perhaps our response to it has.

There is a story of two men walking through a city. Out of nowhere comes a rabid dog.

One man looks at the other and says, "We need to put this dog down!"

The other man responds, "Why? He hasn't done anything wrong!"

"Yes, but he will!"

We are all born on the path of sin, and we all have the sin nature that needs to be "put down" through repentance. Many of us, however, believe repentance isn't needed because of the seemingly good lives we are living. John's voice is being drowned out by the cultural lie that we are good enough apart from Christ.

John got specific when the crowd asked, "What should we do then?" Listen to his response, a call to action: "Anyone who has two shirts should share with the one who has none, and anyone who has food should do the same" (Luke 3:10–11). In other words, care for your neighbor!

John's voice is being drowned out by the cultural lie that we are good enough apart from Christ.

The common themes that run throughout the New Testament are consistent guides. These are not difficult concepts to grasp. They are intentionally delivered in unexpected ways, through humble messengers—repent, love God, love your neighbor. Don't complicate the message. Keep it simple and live it well.

51

Tangible Love

There is a holy sacredness in serving and giving as an act of faith. The effect of a single act can ripple throughout eternity and penetrate deep within one's soul. These acts are a fitting response of our faith, done for our God, through our God, and, strangely, to our God.

Tangible acts of love are not carried out through human strength alone. Moreover, the resulting effects are a mystery understood at the spiritual, soulish level. They begin with concrete acts prepared for us by God, directed toward others (Eph. 2:10). I see these basic expressions of love (Matt. 10:42) creating a connection akin to an electrical circuit between God, you, and your neighbor, with God's power flowing through the circuit and our obedience enabling the flow. We have no power in our own strength, yet our choices open or prevent the flow of God's power. We can accept or reject God's power to run through

> *We have no power in our own strength, yet our choices open or prevent the flow of God's power.*

us. We make choices that either continue the flow or break the circuit.

Jesus declares that the outward manifestation of our inward faith is expressed through action toward our neighbor. These acts always come down to obedience. Noticing the hurting on the side of the road is not enough. We must choose to pause to help or rush past to stay on schedule. Again, loving our neighbor is so high on God's priority list that Jesus says it is like the greatest command—to love God (Matt. 22:39). "Whatever you did for one of the least of these brothers and sisters of mine, you did for me" (Matt. 25:40).

God in us, God in the act, God in our neighbor. God, you, neighbor. This trio reminds me of the Trinity: Father, Son, Holy Spirit. The three live in fellowship with each other, love each other, and honor each other. They are distinct identities living in complete unity, with a deep love and power flowing between them. The fellowship they share was broken only once, and it was in order to repair their connection with humankind.

The restorative work of bridging the connection was carried out by Jesus on the cross. Jesus came to us in a vulnerable way. He came poor, identified with the poor, and came for the poor. Jesus stepped out of glory and "made himself nothing by taking the very nature of a servant, being made in human likeness" (Phil. 2:7).

> "The good news is proclaimed to the poor." (Matt. 11:5)

> "He has anointed me to proclaim good news to the poor." (Luke 4:18)

> Listen, my dear brothers and sisters: Has not God chosen those who are poor in the eyes of the world to be rich in faith and to inherit the kingdom he promised those who love him? (James 2:5)

Is it any wonder there would be for us such a strong connection between God and the vulnerable? Jesus identified with the powerless. In fact, he himself was disenfranchised as a refugee, homeless and transient. Jesus served and cared for his neighbor as an example for us to follow. His love, expressed through meeting practical needs, extended far beyond words. He rocked the religious of his day when he showed them who God considered to be their neighbors: the beaten Jew on the side of road and the Samaritan (an enemy) who cared for him. After this parable, he told them to "Go and do likewise," (Luke 10:37). It is a challenging call to engage with the heart of God's command even when it is counter-cultural, uncomfortable, and inconvenient.

When Jesus returned to glory, he brought his intimate connection with and empathy for the least into the Trinity. Can we be any more like God than when we identify with and serve the poor? This sacred, tangible love mirrors Christ's own actions and obeys his words. His challenging directive to the disciples in Luke 12:33–34 is not lacking in clarity: "Sell your possessions and give to the poor. Provide purses for yourselves that will not wear out, a treasure in heaven that will never fail, where no thief comes near and no moth destroys. For where your treasure is, there your heart will be also."

What could be more in accord with God than to serve and give to our neighbors? Has God not creatively resourced us to meet the needs of those around us? A while back, I got involved in Kid's Hope, a ministry that pairs churches with nearby schools. From there, adults within the church are matched with kids in the school who need extra support. The commitment is to spend time with the child for one hour a week at the school, typically over the lunch hour. When I first started with Kids Hope, I chatted with a woman who had just finished spending an hour with her assigned child. I asked her how this ministry had affected her, and without hesitation she said, "It has changed my life!" Isn't that the way of God's upside down kingdom? We receive more than we give when we give of ourselves. An hour a week reading to, playing games with, talking with and affirming a child can change the course of their life and the life of the giver as well.

The Spirit of God is resident in you, breaking forth with joy and exuberance as you serve. God in you, loving you as you love your neighbor, and your neighbor experiencing tangible love as you obey God in your care for them. Our love for God becomes tangible and visible through our actions toward others. The circular connection is powered by God. God longs for the flow to start and never stop, until we see his Son and the numerous poor becoming rich in glory on that day.

Do we believe enough to love our marginalized neighbor in tangible ways? Do we believe enough to be God's instrument, fully given over to him as our reasonable act of worship (Rom. 12:1)? The premise is clear: loving our neighbor is how both we and they experience God's love. This word picture is described in Matthew 5:14–16: "You are the light of the world. A town built on a hill cannot be hidden. Neither do people light a lamp and put it under a bowl. Instead they put it on its stand, and it gives light to everyone in the house. In the same way, let your light shine before others, that they may see your good deeds and glorify your Father in heaven."

52

Dependent Prayer

I love how honest and vulnerable one of Jesus's disciples was when he asked, "Lord, teach us to pray, just as John taught his disciples" (Luke 11:1). The somewhat curious request came on the heels of Jesus spending time alone in prayer. It must have been strange for the disciples to witness Jesus stealing away to pray.

Of all people, Jesus would seem the least likely to *need* to pray. After all, he was the Son of God and had been with the Father for all eternity past, and he was the one who was behind all creation. Yet not only did he pray, he prayed often, and he prayed alone (Luke 5:16). This need to pray demonstrates the humanity of Jesus and thus his need to regularly tap into the supernatural to receive a fresh filling of the Spirit. Being fully human, Jesus relied on the Spirit of God to lead and guide him (Luke 4:1). We see Jesus modeling an absolute dependence on his Father, and when asked how we should pray, he gives us a dependence-driven prayer.

Jesus was pleased to answer the disciple's question without

judgment, a clear signal that it was a pure and sincere request. Jesus had not directly taught them how to pray before. He modeled prayer and waited for the inquiry before he shared the proper method of prayer. We can learn from this approach, as learning to pray is more caught than taught, as the saying goes. Yet after much modeling, Jesus gets right to the point and lays out a very concise prayer, followed by a parable.

> One day Jesus was praying in a certain place. When he finished, one of his disciples said to him, "Lord, teach us to pray, just as John taught his disciples."
> He said to them, "When you pray, say:
> "'Father, hallowed be your name, your kingdom come. Give us each day our daily bread. Forgive us our sins, for we also forgive everyone who sins against us. And lead us not into temptation.'" (Luke 11:1–4)

The prayer is short, substantive, and restorative. Jesus begins with "Father, hallowed be your name." The prayer begins where we should always begin, by honoring the Father's name—a name above all others, a holy name, fitting of a holy God who is worthy of all honor, glory, and praise.

Next is a succinct yet grandiose request: "Your kingdom come." In Matthew 6:10 Jesus includes, "Your will be done, on earth as it is in heaven." This stops me in my tracks. Isn't God's will accomplished regardless of my prayer? Why would Jesus teach us to pray for his kingdom to come and his will to be done on earth if our prayers don't move the hand of God? While God is sovereign and thus his overarching will is always accomplished, it is a staggering thought to realize we are invited (by Jesus, no less!) to participate in bringing God's will to earth within our sphere or even beyond our sphere.

What a privilege it is to be invited by Jesus to pray for God's will to be accomplished here and now, regardless of not yet knowing the specifics. When we pray in faith for his will to be done, we participate in the transformation. An alignment with the designed will of our heavenly Father happens here on earth. We see an example of a person's faith moving the hand of God in Matthew 9:22: "Your faith has healed you." Too often I associate the earth with all that is wrong (crime, pollution, corruption, greed, hypocrisy ... you get the idea), and yet the model prayer

If he is not giving up on us, his prized creation, then neither should we give up on ourselves.

demonstrates God's desire to align his will with the faith of his followers here on earth. If he is not giving up on us, his prized creation, then neither should we give up on ourselves.

Jesus took this alignment to a level beyond comprehension. He was so perfectly aligned with his Father's will that he only did what he saw his Father doing (John 5:19). I don't pretend to understand the mechanics of that; I only know he was perfectly submissive to his father.

A significant part of his routine was the time he carved out to be in prayer. Even Jesus, who was the Son of God, got away often to pray. How much more do we need to do the same?

Next in the prayer comes the phrase, "Give us each day our daily bread" (Luke 11:3). Jesus shifts here from a gigantic macrorequest of God's will to be done on the earth to a microrequest for one's daily sustenance. This portion of the prayer becomes a request but also a reminder that God is our Provider. In Proverbs, it is addressed this way:

> "Give me neither poverty nor riches, but give me only my daily bread. Otherwise, I may have too much and disown you and say, 'Who is the Lord?' Or I may become poor and steal, and so dishonor the name of my God." (Prov. 30:8–9)

We are so fragile that we need God to help us need God. We need constant reminders of our unceasing dependence on him in order to stay on track. Perhaps it's hard to pray this way because many of us don't currently think we need him for our daily bread. The more we meet our own needs, the less we consider God in our daily rhythms. And yet, we have this prayer from our Lord reminding us to ask for our daily bread, knowing that what God provides will be exactly as much as what we need. "And when they measured it by the omer, the one who gathered much did not have too much, and the one who gathered little did not have too little. Everyone had gathered just as much as they needed" (Exod. 16:18).

Next we are to pray, "Forgive us our sins, for we also forgive everyone who sins against us" (Luke 11:4). We know we have a Savior who is the final sacrifice for our sins, and yet we are to pray for forgiveness as well as the ability to forgive. It seems strange to tie these two together. Of course I need forgiveness for my sins; we all do! Why the link to my forgiveness of everyone who sins against me? Why join something I desperately want for myself to something I don't want to offer those who have wronged me? Yet Jesus ties them together for good reason. How better to experience, albeit in a small way, the price God paid to forgive us than to offer our personal forgiveness to those who have wronged us? This is not just a good idea or a strong suggestion; it is essential to receiving forgiveness. Jesus does not sugarcoat this here or elsewhere. In Matthew 6 he says, "For if you forgive other people when they sin against you, your heavenly Father will also forgive you. But if you do not forgive others their sins, your Father will not forgive your sins" (vv. 14–15).

Finally, Jesus says we ought to pray, "Lead us not into temptation" (Luke 11:4). I must confess one of my biggest temptations is to not forgive those who have wronged me. How interesting, then, we would pray "lead us not into temptation" immediately after we have asked both to receive and to give forgiveness. Jesus, above all others, knew the cost and pain of forgiveness. We see him hanging on the cross asking his Father to forgive his crucifiers (Luke 23:34). We see him taking upon himself the sins of the world, becoming the perfect sacrifice for sin by becoming sin. All of this so forgiveness can be offered.

This last request is for our protection from sin and the destruction that follows. "Lead us not into temptation," Jesus says, and in Matthew 6:13 he adds, "but deliver us from the evil one."

The temptation to sin is all around us and within us. How wonderful to see our Savior recognize this and guide us in this prayer of resistance. Again, we see the pattern of participation. We battle temptation and the evil one from our knees. This is simple and profound. We miss it when we rush past it. We miss it when we don't press into a deep abiding. We miss it when we fail to ask him to lead us away from all that tempts us. God the Father directed Jesus in every way, so much so that Jesus only did what he saw the Father do. Now *that* is abiding. How much more should we abide and press into Jesus's model prayer for protection and deliverance?

How might I embrace the Lord's Prayer and confront my own familiarity with it so as not to miss the rich meaning? Deep contemplation of the words of Jesus always results in deep revelation. His words are spiritually discerned.

I now recognize just how participatory this prayer is. Honoring God, asking in faith for the release of his will and for our sustenance, and now this command that we forgive others in order to be forgiven ourselves. This prayer is anything but a passive ritual.

> *Lord, forgive me for my shallow familiarity with your prayer.*
> *Forgive me for not praying it often.*
> *Forgive me for not applying it well.*

RESOLVE

Forgive me for my lack of forgiveness.
Forgive me for not believing in the power of your will
to change the world.
Thank you for a new day to hallow your name,
to usher in your will,
to trust you for my sustenance,
to accept your forgiveness and
your strength to forgive.
Thank you for leading me away from all that tempts
and for delivering me from the evil one.
Amen.

53

Knowing ≠ Doing

What do you believe enough to do?

−DIETRICH BONHOEFFER−

As Sue approached the front desk, she looked calm and secure, hiding her anxiety just below the surface. She was excited about the interview with Haven Incorporated. She had done her homework and was polished and prepared.

"Welcome," said the man on the other side of the desk. "How can I help you today?"

"I am here to see Mr. Jones about a position."

"Oh yes, he is expecting you. Please have a seat. I will let him know you are here."

As she sat waiting, her mind raced, reviewing all the information she had studied about the company: its origin, history, growth, values, mission, revenue projections, strategic plans, and more. To say she wanted this job was a massive understatement.

She had longed to be part of the Haven team ever since she began her career in the hospitality field.

"You must be Sue," said a gentle voice that came from a tall man in a black suit standing in front of her.

Startled because of how deeply she'd been lost in thought, she replied, "Yes! Yes, I am. Pleased to meet you."

"I'm Mr. Jones. The pleasure is all mine. Come, let's head down to the conference room where we can chat for a while."

Sue was encouraged by Mr. Jones's approachable demeanor. Their conversation flowed smoothly across a wide range of topics.

"I must say, Sue, you have clearly done your homework. You have a tremendous knowledge of our firm. I have not been able to find any area that is lacking in your understanding."

"Why, thank you, Mr. Jones. I have spent a lot of time learning about Haven and conversing with employees of your firm. I have admired Haven for quite some time, especially your stellar reputation. I have a strong desire to be a member of your team. In fact, to be an employee of this organization would be a dream come true."

"Sue, an offer will certainly be extended. You have the foundation we are looking for. Provided you are willing to invest the same time and energy working for Haven as you have in studying about Haven, I see no issues. We have a fabulous team, and so many have shown their commitment through their work and dedicated service to Haven."

"Oh, Mr. Jones, you will not be disappointed in your decision to extend to me this offer," Sue said with enthusiasm and glee.

She was not even out of the lobby before she had phoned her close friend to deliver the exciting news.

"I got the offer!" was heard throughout the atrium. Sue's shy disposition seemed to have evaporated; she wanted the world to know. She was going to be a member of the Haven team!

Over the next few weeks, Sue was sharing her offer from Haven with many. She had the mission statement nailed, knew the detailed history all the way back to the founders. She could tell you the names of the ancestors of the founders. Nothing was lacking in her knowledge of Haven, but Sue missed one thing: she never showed up to work.

All of her knowledge came to nothing because she gave nothing beyond her knowledge.

Somehow, she mistook the offer for the position. She failed to realize the position could only be actualized by showing up. Yes, she believed she was an employee, yet she didn't believe enough to do the work. Rather than stepping into actual service, she gave lip service to her position. All of her knowledge came to nothing because she gave nothing beyond her knowledge.

"You study the Scriptures diligently
because you think that in them you have
eternal life. These are the very Scriptures
that testify about me, yet you refuse to
come to me to have life." (John 5:39–40)

54

Prison, by Choice

We were enjoying a neighborhood get-together at Brian and Christina Aulick's home. Fairly new to the neighborhood and realizing how many neighbors went to their church, the Aulicks (pastors at our church) decided to throw a party to meet each of us. I was standing in the corner of their kitchen grazing on appetizers when Jeff introduced himself. It didn't take long for us to go down the usual conversational lanes of family, career, and friends. Then he began to share a personal tragedy that had shocked and shaped his world. Both of his parents were tragically killed in a car accident a few years prior to this and a big part of his grieving and healing process was to forgive the woman who, while high on marijuana, turned in front of them and took their lives. After numerous months of prayer God softened his heart and prompted him to write her in prison where she was serving time and offered his forgiveness. Later Jeff was asked to share his forgiveness story in a men's prison and while he was there, he discovered the Prison Fellowship Ministry. Intrigued by what he learned, over time he became a volunteer, teaching in the prison each week. "This ministry has changed my life," he stated with conviction.

I had visited a prisoner a number of years ago. That encounter was still fresh in my mind. I had experienced uneasy feelings, even fear, and afterwards an overwhelming sadness for the plight of the young man we visited. I hadn't even entered the prison yard or the cell areas, only the outer visitor section. That was about to change.

Jeff casually invited me to come along with him to check it out. After allowing the request to simmer for a number of weeks, I felt an internal pull to go with him despite the myriad of excuses not to. Honestly, I surprised myself when I texted Jeff to let him know I was interested in tagging along for his next class. I was locked into the commitment, and, as nervous as I was about going, I was even more nervous about where it might lead in my future. Was I going to be committing to a ministry as unconventional and unnerving as a prison ministry? Wouldn't a youth program at church be a better choice? A safer choice? I recalled all the times I had heard the expression, "The safest place to be is in the center of God's will." The problem with that statement is there is nothing even remotely close to that teaching in the New Testament. Rather, true Christ followers lived in the most physically dangerous situations of all. Jesus made it pretty clear that in the world we will have many troubles. He shared that with his disciples who all faced distressing circumstances, and most of them suffered horrific deaths. Many of the chapters in the New Testament were written from a prison cell where the author had been imprisoned *for* being in the center of God's will. Imprisonment *was* the center of God's will.

> "The safest place to be is in the center of God's will." The problem with that statement is there is nothing even remotely close to that teaching in the New Testament.

The dark brown prison structures were surrounded by high walls and fences covered in coils of barbed wire. As Jeff and I walked up to the main entry doors, I couldn't help but see the image of Jesus's crown of thorns repeated again and again draped above the tall chain-link fencing. Jeff made sure I only had my driver's license on my person and even that was taken away from me in exchange for a piece of paper with my visitor ID on it. We passed through four steel sliding doors, each one locking behind us before the next would open. Additionally, we were escorted through a metal detector, endured a pat down, removed our shoes and socks so they could be inspected, tolerated a look under our tongues, and were tagged with a fluorescent mark on the back of our hands, visible only when held under a special light so the guard behind bulletproof glass could see it and approve us to proceed. Lastly, we received a buzzer we connected to our belt. "Press this button if you are in trouble, and guards will come to your rescue," Jeff informed me. *Trouble? What kind of trouble?*

As we walked escorted by a prison guard across the yard to unit six, we met up with Chip, the Academy Program Manager of Prison Fellowship. Near the entry door of the unit was what looked like a makeshift sign resembling a tombstone: Faith Dorm. Chip escorted me, along with another visitor, into the library. We sat on cold, plastic chairs in the somewhat dingy library that felt more like a large closet. Chip invited some prisoners to come in and introduce themselves. Four different individuals dropped in over a forty-five-minute time span. I was taken aback by their cheerful demeanor, articulate speech, and peaceful countenance. Ashamed of my preconceived prejudices, I allowed them to be dismantled one by one.

While I can't recall all that was said in those moments, a few statements stuck with me:

> We know we are on the bottom rung of the social ladder. We see you as laying down your life for us and humanizing us through your visit. In this place we

are serious about how we live for Christ and how we serve each other. We are serious doers of the word.

They shared with us their stories, rich with redemption and praise for Christ who had made the difference—all the difference—for them. I felt a deep connection to these men, men I had just met, whom I had so little in common with. But I felt the presence of God's spirit in that space, in their eyes, in their voices. How could men such as these, with hearts transformed by Christ, with such deep maturity, be in this place? In prison, society had put them out of sight and for the most part out of mind. I felt a deep burden for them as I walked out of there that day. I knew this was not the last time I would see them or be in this *not* God-forsaken place. I asked myself if I could ever recall being with a group of men who had such depth of devotion these men seemed to have? I came up empty.

I wondered why I felt such a profound connection to this place. A feeling came over me, a feeling I belonged here. A feeling these were my brothers. In time, I became a registered Prison Fellowship volunteer and began teaching my own class each week.

As I consider my life, my mistakes, my losses, my choice of ending a life—I belong in this place, yet I am free. I carry, however, the burden of their imprisonment in my heart. They are imprisoned yet have a newfound freedom in Christ. It is a privilege to be with them each week in this season of my life. What they do for me trumps what I do for them. Each man is unique, each with their own story, each at different levels of recovery and discovery. Each one is special.

I had a new class just this week and told the men I was there because I didn't want to waste my life. I hadn't planned to say that, it just came out. It was sincerely how I felt. Whenever we invest in the "least of these," we discover they are anything but. I have found spiritual giants within those walls, men that put my walk to shame, and men I am proud to call my brothers. Many have overcome incredibly difficult life circumstances on their way to their eternal redemption.

> "Therefore, I tell you, her many sins have been
> forgiven—as her great love has shown." (Luke 7:47)

55

A Flawed Hero

The darkness is the hardest part. I never realized how much sight was a distraction, distracting me from facing my sin. Funny how, when I could see, I was blind to my sin; yet now that I'm blind, my sin is visibly before me. It plays out in living color across the stage of my mind.

I would never have imagined myself here. Not in a hundred lifetimes. But this is where I find myself—my eyes gouged out, pushing against this large wood lever, listening to the grain grinding with each painful step. Stopping even for a moment is met with a strike from a Philistine guard. These guards live to mock and torment me. Why shouldn't they? I spent much of my life tormenting and embarrassing them with defeat after defeat, death after death. I'm sure I've killed one of their friends or loved ones along the way. Why I am permitted to live is a mystery. Keeping me alive as a spectacle is, I suppose, a more fitting punishment. They are making a spectacle of the one who spent his life making a spectacle of the Philistines.

At times when the guards are silent, I hear the passersby, sometimes children. Usually they laugh, sometimes they throw garbage my way or even spit on me. Of course, I hate this, but it's better than the silence. Yes, the silence is a much greater torture, for in the silence I torture myself by swirling within my past. Those *what ifs* and *if onlys* haunt me here. I replay critical points of my life, each poor decision I have made and how it led me here to this awful place of perpetual torment. My life is over. My extraordinary life has come to this humiliating end.

Where would I be had I made different decisions? What if I had lived into my calling rather than abused it? What if I had used my extraordinary, God-given strength solely for God's glory and God's victory instead of my own? What if I had not listened to and lusted after the enticing tempters that crossed my path. I knew better. My body was strong, but my mind and will were, oh, so weak. I lived a self-deceived life. I had equated my abilities and gifts with God's favor on my life. How foolish I was to believe blessing and favor were one and the same! I believed I was not accountable as long as I was able to achieve success by winning the battles before me and keeping the Philistines at bay.

> I had equated my abilities and gifts with God's favor on my life.

Yet now it is clear to me. Now the accumulation of my poor choices and the accumulation of sin weigh so heavily upon me. Now it is clear.

Still though, with each new breath I take, I have hope. For I was given this opportunity to reunite with the God of my youth.

It was here, on this grinding floor, where he met me again—this time, in my weakness and shame. I was at the end of myself, pathetic and irrelevant. Oddly, I felt that God desired to meet here, where he is strong instead of me, where he is the victor instead of me, where he can be heard now that my loud and selfish ways have been silenced.

I spend my remaining days in communion with him. My faith grows on this grinding floor. My faith, right along with the grain, is refined as I walk in circle after circle after circle, praying with each step. I found my way back to great faith, but this time my faith is in him alone. I confess my sin and allow his forgiveness to wash over me. His warmth and his presence are tangible.

Eventually he leads me to my final act, slowly restoring my physical strength in preparation. However, this time is different. This time I wait on him, his direction, his prompting.

Suddenly I am pulled out of the grinding floor by two Philistine guards, one on each side. Where am I heading? The faint noise of voices in the distance amplifies as we reach the steps of the structure that houses a large gathering. The smell of wine mingled with other fragrances is intoxicating as we make our way up the stairs. I am used to laughter, but this is different. An ocean of voices indicates this is a massive gathering and I have been summoned to be the entertainment. The opening scene is a slap across my face. Raucous jeering erupts from the crowd.

"You didn't see that coming did you?"

"Not so mighty now, huh!"

"Prophesy for us, big man!"

In days past, I would have filled with rage. But now, empathy is all I feel. And prayer—constant prayer—is all I can think to do. My time is short. I simply want it to end.

Directed by God, I pull the hand of one of the guards and whisper, "Please take me to the main pillar so that I might lean against it." He obliges, a sign that God is directing this.

The crowd still mocks me with full-throated laughter. I know they worship a dragon god of their own making. To them, my capture is evidence he is real and lives to give them victory.

The guard directs my right hand to the pillar. With my left hand, I reach out to the adjacent pillar. I pray my final prayer of faith.

"Sovereign Lord, remember me. Please, God, strengthen me just once more, and let me with one blow get revenge on the Philistines for my two eyes. . . . Let me die with the Philistines!" (Judg. 16:28, 30).

He hears me, and I rejoice in him as my weakness turns to strength. His power flows through me one last time. I push the pillars outward and turn my head upward. I was blind but soon I will see.

I have carried the story of Samson through my most difficult times. For me, the story has gone far beyond the historical record of this Nazarene's life. I see Samson as a flawed hero whose life echoes across time, reverberating the message of second chances, hope, and deliverance. I have reflected deeply on his life and the many poor choices that filled him with regret. Moreover, I have reflected deeply on the forgiveness, redemption, and restoration he experienced. His story has filled me with a fresh hope and assurance. How can anyone read about this man and feel that God is out of reach or that God has given up on us? God came near to him in his contrite, broken state. God washed him of his sin. God restored his strength and gave him the greatest victory of his lifetime before taking him home. I look at Samson and see his name written in the coveted hall of faith in Hebrews 11. I'm filled with hope for my life. For I, too, have sinned. I, too, have blown it. I, too, have not measured up to the potential of a Spirit-filled believer. Yet I see hope ahead of me with each new breath. I soak in the hope of Samson, and as I do, I feel a renewed strength, a renewed cleansing, a renewed courage to answer God's calling. I'm thankful for this man who got it right in the end and who calls us to the same—not looking back but pressing on to our greatest victory, just ahead, and the greatest defeat of the enemies of our soul. Satan, the accuser of believers, and his demons will in the end be silenced by Christ. Yes, Christ, the greatest hero of all, will take away our sin, wash us clean, and remove our enemies in like fashion to what he did through Samson.

> And what more shall I say? I do not have time to
> tell about Gideon, Barak, Samson and Jephthah,
> about David and Samuel and the prophets,
> who through faith conquered kingdoms,
> administered justice, and gained what was
> promised; who shut the mouths of lions, quenched
> the fury of the flames, and escaped the edge
> of the sword; whose weakness was turned to
> strength; and who became powerful in battle
> and routed foreign armies. (Heb. 11:32–34)

56

I Love Jesus

I love how Jesus came for sinners.

I love that he chose to be poor.

I love how Jesus unmasked hypocrisy.

I love how Jesus spoke truth regardless of the fallout.

I love that Jesus was tempted in every way but didn't sin.

I love that he was willing to take the risk of being tempted.

I love how Jesus covered himself in prayer, and often got away
alone to pray to his Father.

I love how Jesus now lives to intercede on our behalf to the Father.

I love how he is slow to anger.

I love how Jesus came to serve rather than be served.

I love how he spoke in parables the simple can understand and
intellectuals can ponder for years.

I love how Jesus, Creator of all that is, lived a simple life.

I love how he laid down his life for me and took it up again
to bring me home.

I love how he alone can demand total and unashamed devotion
to himself and his body, the church. For he gave total devotion
to his Father and died for his church (us).

I love how he loved.

I love that he cried.

I love that he loved us enough to warn us about hell.

I love that he got mad.

I love that he was meek and not weak.

I love how he forgave the most unforgivable of sins and sinners.

I love that he called me to be full of mercy, full of love, full of
forgiveness, and I love that I can't do that on my own but that
I can through faith in him.

I love how he loved his Father and relied on him.

I love that he took all my sin and blotted it out to be remembered
no more.

I love how Jesus silences the accuser of my soul because he already
paid the penalty for my sin.

I love how he guides me in becoming more like him through his
Spirit that resides within me.

I love that I will be with him forever and that he calls me his
friend.

I love that I, through prayer, have direct access to the Father
because of his crazy sacrifice.

I love how the little things didn't escape his attention then and
how they don't now, even in my simple life.

I love how he pursues me and brings me back when I wander. I
even love the pain of his discipline, for in that pain I feel loved
(Ps. 119:71).

I love him in so many ways, and I love that I have this new day to
pursue obedience, allegiance, mercy, forgiveness, and grace
one more time.

I love that even though I will come up short, he has my shortfall
covered for me.

I love that his yoke is easy and his burden is light.

I wish the world knew him better. I wish I were a better
ambassador for him. And yet . . . I love that he provides
me with new chances to represent him well—today
and every day!

57

Crazy Path of Faith

As my fifty-eighth birthday approaches, it feels fitting to take a step back and broadly survey the terrain of my life as a Christ follower. I am fortunate on many levels, and soon I will celebrate a milestone my father never experienced. I am grateful to have found Christ at a relatively early age and don't take it for granted my faith is still intact. From my father to me, and now from Chris and I to our children, this faith is not just my own, it is part of the tapestry of our family. I'm fortunate to have married a woman who lives her faith authentically and has supported me and her children in prayer throughout the years.

I recognize this faith journey is long, full of potholes and distractions and, at times, discomfort and outright pain. Faith is exercised, developed, and grown most often though trials and hardships. Unfortunately, many people abandon their faith or walk away for a season (as I have) out of misplaced anger at God for allowing such things to happen. These hardships are sometimes brought on by sinful choices that lead to retreating from God to hide one's shame. At other times, these seasons are by-products of a broken world and our messy lives which can make navigating them even more arduous.

In addition, the faith journey can be confusing. A respected pastor falls into sin, a family member behaves hurtfully, a friend walks away from the faith—all of these can leave us feeling disillusioned and disappointed. When faith becomes confusing, it is so easy to allow Jesus to shrink into the background of life and only to acknowledge him in safe compartments like Sunday morning or in a particular group of friends. Refusing to recognize that Jesus exists in the midst of our questions and tensions only limits our understanding of him as a savior and redeemer. I regularly have to remind myself that I am looking at imperfect people and not my perfect Lord. I have to invite him into my disappointments and allow him to bring healing and wholeness and not expect that from the world around me.

Finally, I understand how the faith journey is especially challenging during seasons of doubt. At times, I have questioned my own beliefs or the faith of those around me. Is it real and genuine or just a show? How do I know for sure? At times my kids have brought doubts forward, and I wished I had better answers for them. Like the time our second son Josh asked, "Dad, if I were born in China, I would most likely be a Buddhist and a sincere one. How do I know Christianity is legit?" These questions are real, valid, and should be welcomed as a part of our journey. But our lack of answers does not indicate a lack of God. I am less certain now, yet somehow more comfortable with the uncertainty. I have so few answers to my ever-growing list of questions, but Jesus has become the only answer I need, my bedrock. More than ever, I recognize the importance of God's Word in grounding me to what is true about him. Returning to the

I have gotten sidetracked and have wasted the only commodity I can never retrieve: my time.

truth has allowed me to navigate seasons of doubt without losing my footing.

Too often—too many times to count—I have gotten sidetracked and have wasted the only commodity I can never retrieve: my time. This year has caused me to reflect on the people in my life, not the accomplishments or accumulations. I have learned to live in the present, in this very day. It is not about living on the laurels of yesterday's faith or dwelling on yesterday's failures. Neither is it about tomorrow and my hope to get things "right." I cannot always peer forward toward moments that may never happen or be granted to me. Faith is always best expressed in the present. "Today, if you hear his voice, do not harden your hearts," it says in Hebrews 4:7. It is so important for me to view each moment as precious and valuable. Paul reminds us to "make the most of every opportunity" (Col. 4:5). After all, "What is your life? You are a mist that appears for a little while and then vanishes" (James 4:14). When the brevity-of-life perspective lapses, I so easily settle into unintentional patterns or make faithless decisions that hurt others. My fifty-seventh year of life has rooted me deep into purpose, gratitude, and an overriding appreciation for God's grace.

Over the course of writing this book, I have found deeper meaning and peace for my soul. This was not true just a few years back when I found myself in a restless state, trying to balance an insanely busy work schedule, chasing success in business, and attempting to grow my faith. I sought out ways to become more involved through volunteering and serving in my local community—all good things, but not so good if they're done out of obligation or burden. I had frustrations with the larger church in America because I didn't feel it was teaching the full truth or providing what was needed. I was internally churning as I sought out solutions, answers. I found myself hanging out with ex-pastors who were equally frustrated. We could commiserate for hours about what was wrong with Christianity in our country and debate what the biblical structure of the church should look like, or at least our version of it.

This past year of reflection, however, has brought about a change within me. I am allowing God more room to breathe into my life and inviting him to show up in nonprescribed ways, even within the imperfect structures where his people gather. I am learning to control my fix-it tendencies and to live into my personal call to revive love for God and my neighbor. The power of generosity continues to blow my mind. Scripture is chock-full of example after example of benefits for the generous: benefits of heavenly rewards; benefits of imparted righteousness; benefits to those you are helping; benefits of joy; benefits of a lighter, less burdensome life. But in the end, all I have and all I am is because of Christ.

This year may have been burdened by grief, but it was also rich with hope. Hope in new life, hope in resurrection, hope in the power of God to reveal himself to us, forgive us, and partner with us. Each day of this year was an exercise in not only looking backward at the times he was unmistakably faithful but also gazing to the future with resolve. A new level of commitment to truth, love, and action has stirred within me. I resolve to be more present with my Savior, to be more generous to my neighbor, to be bolder with the truth, and to be more expectant of the miraculous. I resolve to be a voice in the wilderness, a help to the hurting, and a friend even to my foes. Won't you join me?

> The Word became flesh and made his dwelling
> among us. We have seen his glory, the glory
> of the one and only Son, who came from the
> Father, full of grace and truth. (John 1:14)

ACKNOWLEDGMENTS

There are some people I would like to specifically thank who were directly or indirectly part of *Resolve*.

My wife, Chris, for understanding my incessant drive to write and reflect over this year, along with her stories and prayers that I would finish!

Karyl Morin, my friend who became my writing coach: for her direction, edits, encouragement, and godly counsel throughout this project.

My children: David, Josh, Seth, Luke, and Grace. Each have impacted my life in so many ways and have woven their stories within mine.

My sister, Karyn Lee, for being vulnerable and allowing me to share her stories that have impacted my life in so many ways.

My sister, Karyl DeBruyn, for planting the seed for a book with fifty-seven reflections.

Carolyn Buck for her work in shaping the structure, final edits, title, and subtitle.

Those who read and critiqued the manuscript: Grace Bakker, Rob Flint, Micah Kephart, Berny Bennett, Jim and Mary Zuidema (my awesome in-laws), and Chad Allen.

My staff for their understanding when I had to carve out time to work on this project.

My parents, Karl and Marie, whose passing became the impetus for this book, and their faith that has shaped my life.